Bread 1,00

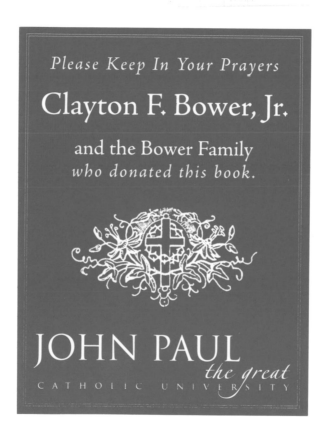
History
900

COLUMBUS, SPAIN, AND THE INCAS

COLUMBUS, SPAIN, AND THE INCAS

*A Brief Historical Narrative of the Great
Discovery
and the Spanish Conquest, Celebrating a
Half-Millennium of America,
1492-1992*

Theodore Carlos Combs

Illustrated by Erika Oller

VANTAGE PRESS
New York

FIRST EDITION

Copyright © 1992 by Theodore Carlos Combs

Published by Vantage Press, Inc.
516 West 34th Street, New York, New York 10001

Manufactured in the United States of America
ISBN: 0-533-09691-X

Library of Congress Catalog Card No.: 91-91023

0 9 8 7 6 5 4 3 2 1

To the memory of my dear wife, Carmen. Like Columbus, we ventured into many lands previously unknown to us. Our life was an exciting adventure with family and friends, organizations, reading, writing, and assisting worthwhile causes.

Contents

Preface

Early in 1986, my wife Carmen and I visited Santiago, Chile, en route home from Antarctica. Our hotel was about a block from the Catedral de San Francisco (Saint Francis Cathedral). We visited its museum and were surprised to see some fifty large oil paintings depicting the life of St. Francis of Assisi. We were even more surprised to be informed that these were painted by Indians, in the 1500s, in an art school in Cuzco. They are allegedly the oldest such paintings in the Western Hemisphere.

The figures and clothing in these paintings are representative of the finest of sixteenth century art, as if they had been painted in Rome or Paris. Certainly, Indians in upper Peru would have had no concept of the raiment, hairstyles, and complexions—or even the various episodes of the life of St. Francis. They conceivably might have applied paints to cartoons under the guidance of an expert. Documentation available to us was meager. Being inquisitive, I was left with a variety of questions. And questions demand answers.

I had previously visited Cuzco and, in fact, much of Peru, Colombia, and Bolivia, and had some appreciation of the advanced Inca civilization—but the origin of those paintings didn't fit in. From this came a resolve to search for more information.

Fortunately, I live in a community having excellent libraries. Reading narratives of the Spanish discovery, conquest, and development of the western world soon broadened into research of a much wider scope. Mild interest became deep interest and then a compulsion. One invaluable resource was the Huntington Library where I had had a readership for several years. Imagine being able to study facsimiles of original letters written in the late 1400s and early 1500s, and authorizations signed by Queen Isabella and King Ferdinand. One reference is a book published by the library itself. Only one hundred copies were printed. But although there are myriad books on related subjects, there was no one book that told the story I wanted to read. Perhaps, I thought, I should compile it.

Fortunately, also, I had read several historical novels unrelated to the present subject. I appreciated how normally dull history can come alive through the resourcefulness of an imaginative author. So, rudimentary thoughts of writing a book developed into a conviction that it had to be a historical narrative. I say "narrative" because this story does not have the ponderous length of a historical novel, but it does have some fictional dialog.

There came hesitation over whether I should undertake such a task. My prior writing had been mostly technical. Then I remembered my grandfather telling me of his friend Lew Wallace who, an unknown author, wrote *Ben Hur*, a tremendous success. Wallace, a retired Army officer, became governor of the Territory of New Mexico, 1878–81, where Granddad knew him at the time *Ben Hur* was being written. Wallace didn't consider his writing as work, but as enjoyment. That recollection convinced me to go ahead. I have enjoyed the experience tremendously.

The world will focus its attention on Columbus and the development of the Western Hemisphere during the five hundredth anniversary of his discovery. We will celebrate the beginning of a New World. Hopefully, this treatise can enhance your appreciation of events that changed the world. And we might learn more about those paintings.

Introduction

It should be noted that the entire text is in English except where Spanish or Peruvian terms are inserted because they add color or appreciation. In those instances, equivalents are added where appropriate. Foreign names are given in the original language for consistency with the works of other authors.

Diligent effort has been exercised to report actual facts accurately. Fiction is not expressly identified, but should be apparent to the reader. Fiction is, however, intended to be realistic.

Several rereadings of manuscript should have eliminated errors. It seems inevitable, however, that some errors may not have been detected, for which I apologize and request that I be advised of them.

Especial gratitude is expressed to the authors of the many books cited in the Bibliography. Their seemingly endless research and writing has provided a highly detailed record of one of the most fascinating and significant periods of world history.

In most books, the archaeologist has stayed with archaeology and the historian has stayed with history. My interest in getting back to sources and "reasons why" has led me into several fields: geology, mineralogy, oceanography, navigation, shipbuilding, and several others. I have enjoyed being venturesome. I hope it has enriched your understanding and appreciation.

Continued reference to Western Hemisphere natives as "Indians" has always seemed inappropriate to me. In fact, it has caused misunderstandings and is scorned by the people of India. I use the word "natives" or some synonym.

Although the Incas were the chieftains of the tribes of Peru and neighboring areas, I have fallen into the habit of thinking of Incas as being both the rulers and the ruled. Please forgive such freedom.

I am grateful to artist Erika Oller for her excellent illustrations. Aren't they splendid?

COLUMBUS, SPAIN, AND THE INCAS

Chapter 1

An Idea Takes Shape

"Bartholomew, I've been thinking." Christopher Columbus was talking to his younger brother. "Here we are in
Genoa, where there is no hope for our dreams to come
true. You are a map maker, and selling maps here in
Italy has little prospect. Thanks to Father's training, I
am a skilled weaver, but that trade doesn't interest me.
Anyhow, Father has never prospered and our family has
always been poor. I love boats and navigating, so I make
a living with the fishing fleet. But I'd like to be more
venturesome and do some exploring like the Portuguese.
I'd like to go over the horizon, but those stupid fishermen
refuse to get out of sight of land. I think we should go to
Portugal where the action is."

"My dear brother, I have been thinking, too—much
the same as you. But leaving our family would be difficult. And how do we know we could make a living? Yes,

Prince Henry the Navigator established a great school. It became a world center for navigators and astronomers and instrument makers and cartographers. But he died fifteen years ago. The school continues, but no one today is as great as Prince Henry. You are right, though. The Portuguese are explorers and are discovering new lands along the African coast. But even they refuse to get out of sight of land. Oh, there are exceptions. They found the Azores. I hear they are searching out a route to the Indies by following the African coast. Perhaps some day the tortuous Silk Road will no longer be needed."

"Now you've put your finger on something, Bartholomew. I've been studying. I'm convinced that the Portuguese are wrong, and I'd like to prove it. The logical route to the Indies is westerly and not around Africa. You know what Aristotle said—that one could cross the Ocean Sea to the Indies in a few days. No one has ever dared argue with Aristotle. And I know you have seen Ptolemy's maps, because they are being republished in Rome. His knowledge of the world has never been disputed in more than a thousand years. As the inventor of latitude and longitude, he improved all subsequent maps and charts."

"But Ptolemy's maps, using his own longitude, show only half the world."

"Of course, silly. The other half is all sea. There's no use having blank space on a map just to show all 360 degrees. But you have studied his map. Certainly the most direct route to Asia is to the west. Anyhow, Marco Polo gave encouragement to mariners without realizing it. Two hundred years ago, when writing about the Silk Road, he pointed out that Cipangu (Japangu) is a thousand Roman miles east of China. It is the closest to here, so I'd like to make it my first port of call."

"As a map maker, dear Christopher, I have perhaps

2

seen more charts than you. There is the Hereford Mappa Mundi of 1280. And Brother Mauro's world map of 1459. I could name others. But none of them helps your objective. How about restudying Marco Polo?"

"Fabulous person, he, Bartholomew. I have already restudied him. His tremendously difficult route, full of hazards, convinced me that a sea route must be found. Marco succeeded despite many obstacles. I hope we can. Our biggest obstacle will be to find someone to provide funds for ships and crews and provisions. I proposed this to the Senate here in Genoa. I told them they should be the first to claim new lands and untold riches. What did they do? They appointed a committee. The committee studied the matter. And studied. And studied. They finally came up with a report—nearly a thousand pages of nothingness. They patted themselves on the back. They suggested further study—at government expense, I suppose. Without saying so, they discouraged westward exploration. But you'll be interested in this: when Dr. Tagletti of the University of Milan became ill and couldn't attend meetings, a young engineer named Leonardo da Vinci was named to sit in for him. One of the members told me he was really eccentric. He talked about flying machines and fancied himself an artist. They thought he was immature and had poor judgment, for he highly favored the voyage. I visited him later and found him to be highly perceptive. I wish he had been a little older and better known. He might have been more persuasive."

Bartholomew asked, "Do you suppose the pope in Rome might help?"

"I tried to arrange an audience with Pope Sixtus IV. He is a Franciscan, devoted to the teachings of Saint Francis of Assisi. But his two compelling interests are the rebuilding of Rome and the construction of the Sistine

Chapel, together with gaining positions and favors for members of his family. I didn't qualify and he didn't find time to see me."

After several months the two brothers decide to move to Portugal. Bartholomew went first. In Lisbon he opened a chart-making establishment and became acquainted with others of like interests.

Christopher, meanwhile, had been on some long voyages and had improved his navigational skill. He was a mature thirty. He met an attractive young lady in church and soon married her, Donna Felipa, of one of the first families of Portugal. She bore him a son whom they named Ferdinand. Unfortunately, after a few years, she died. And although it was not easy, Christopher gave his son good schooling and saw that he received proper care. He maintained relationships with Donna's family and, through them, knew Portuguese leaders.

One of these contacts was provident. A distant relative of Prince Henry the Navigator, King John II, encouraged navigators and cartographers in the tradition of Henry. Through John's encouragement, Portuguese possessions on the African coast brought prosperity—but not enough to support a westward exploration; nor did they feel that going west would be as rewarding as continuing their African explorations. So, Christopher must wait. He did, however, continue to receive encouragement, such as an unexpected letter from Leonardo da Vinci, who had continued to think about their meeting. Leonardo had read Marco Polo's book, a hand-copied edition scripted before the age of printing. He had also made some scientific deductions. He urged his friend to continue to attempt to establish that new route to the land of silks.

Chapter 2
Spain in the 1400s

To appreciate the life and times confronting Columbus
when he was seeking support for his great adventure,
one must understand Spain during the 1400s. Over the
centuries it had been a no-man's land—or, more accurately, everyman's land.

Early on, Spain was a victim of contention between
Carthage and Rome. Even Hannibal of Carthage
marched up through the Spanish peninsula with his ele-
phants, through the Pyrenees, over the Alps, and down
toward Rome. Finally, the Romans dominated, but
whereas they had needed only seven years to conquer
Gaul, they needed two centuries for Hispania. Meanwhile, there was an influx of Greeks and Phoenicians.
Then Christianity arrived in the first century A.D., thanks
to Roman tolerance. Peace? No. Christianity was not
peaceful in those days.

From the North came Vandals, Visigoths, and others. The Romans had given the Jews a free hand and they prospered in Spain. The Moors of North Africa were invited in for stability. They brought their new religion, Mohammedanism, and they stayed. Soon they controlled much of Spain, though Catholicism prospered in the North. Gradually, the Moors were forced south and based themselves in Cordova and Granada. Then Spain fragmented into seven different jurisdictions, one of which was the County of Portugal which became an independent kingdom with monarchs interrelated with the Spanish.

In the cities particularly, the Spaniards learned to live by their wits, preferring royal favors to honest work. Moral values went to pot. An office seeker might double-cross a member of his family in seeking an appointment. The custom of bloodline succession among royalty resulted in some inept rulers and influenced marriages based solely on political considerations. Catholicism gained strength, and the Pope and his bishops and friars were not always exemplary to their flocks. They talked openly about their offspring.

Take the case of Rodrigo Borgia. He was actually Rodrigo Llanco who assumed the name of his uncle of that name when his uncle became Pope Alexander VI. He knew full well that his countrymen prided themselves on their number of exotic mistresses and bragged about their prowess. He knew that the height of achievement for a lady of high position was a retinue of "suitors" and that she compared notes with others as to their quality. With no birth-control measures or abortions, the population of illegitimate children rose alarmingly. The Pope did take steps—he legitimized the bastards in families where it was politically important to do so, for, by law, only legitimate offspring could inherit property or become royalty.

He also knew that members of the clergy were no exception to male indulgences, himself included. Not all scholars agree as to the morals of Alexander VI, in view of his many brilliant achievements otherwise. It is probable that he was a great achiever in more than one direction.

Legitimacy had complications in high places. Example: Isabella's half-brother Enrique (Henry) was apparently impotent. This didn't impede his becoming King, however. After some lapse of time his second wife, Juana of Portugal, produced a daughter who was also named Juana. Court scuttlebutt, among those who knew Juana's comings and goings, was that young Juana was illegitimate. Came the question as to whether she might legally succeed Henry to the throne. And might she marry other royalty? Ask the Pope.

This was no time for intellectual achievements or humor. Works like that of Cervantes and his *Don Quixote* would not appear for several generations.

The Jews were honest and able and achieved important positions. Their very success aroused the envy and hatred of others. Anyhow, Jews were not Christians. Attempts were made to convert them or oust them. Some accepted baptism and became devout Catholics. Others went through the motions but maintained their Jewish faith. But most remained Jews despite indignities and physical punishment.

The Moors dominated southern Spain. They had been there so long that cities like Cordova and Granada had achieved architectural grandeur unsurpassed anywhere. They were successful in their trades. Their Moslem world was one to be envied. But they, too, were not

Christians and to the Catholics of Castile they were impostors.

This was virtual chaos. This was the Spanish world that Columbus entered. It was also the world that Isabella inherited.

———

Chapter 3
Isabella — Magnificent

Make a list of women who have contributed most to the world. Then, if it is not already there, place the name of Queen Isabella of Spain at the top. Let's consider why. Her achievements must be related to the life and times of her era. In the mid-1400s Spain was virtually bankrupt, morally and financially. She reunited its provinces and brought her country to world prominence. She inherited a country of opposing religions and converted it to Christianity. She backed an unknown mariner in whom she believed, and gained the New World. Four of her five children became distinguished royalty. Her mate was often less than helpful, yet she maintained her poise, her leadership for her country, and her devotion to him. And she was beautiful.

Isabella grew up without a father. King Juan II of Castile had died when she was three. She lacked the loving care of a mother, for she was sent to the Convent of Santa Ana in Avila. Her father had been a widower with an adolescent son, Enrique (Henry) when he married Isabel of Portuguese royalty. They soon produced two children—Isabella and Alfonso. Henry never developed a close relationship with his half-sister. Alfonso and Isabella were friendly youngsters, but Alfonso became an enemy in later years when he was King of Portugal.

The convent provided Isabella with exceedingly fine care and education, for it was realized that she might someday become a queen. She developed character, an appreciation of the views of others, a knowledge of the history of Spain and its neighbors, and a special devotion to Catholicism. Would that we knew about her instructors. Alas, history does not even record their names. Like so many excellent teachers, they remained anonymous.

Henry had become king, succeeding his father in royal tradition. But he was not ready for the responsibility. Spain, under his rule, began to disintegrate. So did Henry, sinfully. He disposed of his stepmother (Isabella's mother) by having her declared insane. Fearing that Isabella might displace him, he tried to sidetrack her by arranging for her marriage to Alfonso V, King of Portugal, a distant relative. Isabella would have none of it. By this time she was a mature seventeen. When offered the crown she had refused it, contending that it should be returned to Henry, as he was more entitled to it than she. She also confided in her advisers that a marriage to Fernando of Aragon would be politically suitable.

Fernando (we will now call him Ferdinand) was heir to the throne of Aragon. The possibility of uniting their two countries had a potent potential, for they were both

Catholic and might unify Spain as a Catholic country. The Archbishop of Toledo agreed (or perhaps he originated the idea). Ferdinand was willing, but needed time because his country was engaged in a war. King Henry learned of the arrangement and was incensed. He dispatched a military force to take Isabella into custody. Fearing dire consequences, she appealed to the Bishop of Toledo for assistance. The Bishop who, of course, had no army, sent out an appeal for help. Three hundred horsemen responded. En route to Madrigal two hundred more joined in. Henry's detachment, seeing that it was overwhelmed, retired.

Meanwhile, Isabella had been transferred to Valladolid, wearing a disguise to avoid detection. There, Ferdinand, also wearing a disguise and having passed through Henry's force, arrived to meet his bride-to-be. What a circumstance for two teenagers! She was eighteen. He was seventeen. His father had just awarded him the crown of Aragon as a wedding present. On October 19, 1467, they were married by the archbishop. There was dancing in the streets to celebrate the most popular marriage in anyone's memory.

King Henry behaved badly. Public rebellion ensued and he was forced to relent. Then he became ill following a dinner and died. Poisoned by a malcontent, perhaps?

Isabella decided to be crowned at once. Ferdinand was not present, having had to return to Aragon to contend with an invasion. When he returned he was enraged that she had accepted the sword of justice, a male tradition. The cardinal and the archbishop resolved the argument and succeeded in negotiating a workable understanding. She, of dominant Castile, would make all decisions, but not until she had consulted with him. He was to be King by courtesy only. They would reside in Castile. Together, they would Catholicize the Jews or oust them. They would continue the holy war against the Moors. He, following the custom of the times, might have mistresses. (According to the record he fathered five bastards.) What an understanding! It was apparent that they were vastly different in temperament and outlook. Isabella was destined to have many a rough moment.

Then King Alfonso of Portugal got into the act—Isabella's own half-brother! He claimed that he, the male heir, was automatically King of Castile. He declared war and his army of twenty thousand marched into Castile to lay claim. Queen Isabella donned armor and appealed to Castilians for support. What a distressful time for the young queen! Overexerting, she miscarried. Two days later she was campaigning again. An "army" of sixty thousand assembled, outnumbered Alfonso's, and forced a retreat.

Now the top item was the Jew. To that date the Inquisition had had only limited success despite thousands of tortures and burnings at the stake. The queen and king issued an order: become baptized Christians or leave the country. Thus began a merciless crusade, fomented by court advisers such as Torquemada, the Grand Inquisitor. The Pope approved. Next would be the Moors.

Gradually, Spain became one of the strongest states in Europe, though its coffers were always nearly empty. Enter Christopher Columbus in 1485. He had already spent eleven years seeking support for his great adventure. But how could he make headway in Spain, in view of its major commitments and lack of resources? He managed to gain an audience with Their Majesties. Isabella, handsome and perceptive, expressed interest. Ferdinand had his mind on other things. The proposal dangled, but Isabella—and thereby hangs a tale worthy of a separate book. The capsulized version is that Columbus finally prevailed despite a series of encouragements/discouragements. Funding was provided for ships, crews, and provisions. He was awarded the titles that had been such a hangup during negotiations: Admiral of the Ocean Sea, Viceroy and Governor of new territories, and an entitlement to be known as Don Cristobal Colon. He was permitted to retain a tenth of all gold, etc., etc., tax-free. He was to introduce Catholicism into the new lands.

By 1504 Isabella had become ill and was preparing for death, although she was only fifty-three. In making final arrangements she provided for Ferdinand and succession to the throne. She was concerned over the plight of the natives of the Indies and ordered kindly treatment. Thinking of others rather than herself, she wished for a better Christian world. Though her escutcheon was loaded with achievements, she realized that there was still much unfinished business. She died October 12, 1504, exactly twelve years after the discovery of America, concerned over her unsolved problems to the very last.

Philip had died and Juana had become really insane. Queen Isabella's six-year-old grandson, Charles, was rightfully heir to the throne, so Ferdinand became regent in his behalf.

A major concern had been the proper settlement and Christianization of the New World. When Columbus had returned with natives to sell as slaves to defray his expenses, Isabella was adamant that this never occur. She censured the Great Discoverer. She was also deeply disappointed that he had not taken a friar on his first voyage. She had never felt that things were going according to her wishes and instructions.

Certainly if any person ever warranted sainthood,

Isabella did. And apparently she was so recognized. There is a carving at the Convent of Santa Ana: "Isabel of Castile—Sainted. In this monastery was educated the young Princess Isabel who went out from Avila to become the Catholic Majesty, forger of Great Spain."

Chapter 4

The Pizarro Boys

Four Pizarro boys. Street-wise. Future ruffians, growing up in Trujillo, Estremadura, Southwest Spain. In order of age, their names were Hernando, Francisco, Juan, and Gonzales. Hernando was born just after his father, Gonzalo senior, was married. The other three boys were products of extramarital unions. There is only a meager record of their mother or mothers. Francisco's mother was Francisca Morales, who apparently ceased being Gonzalo's bedfellow early on. Perhaps it was the custom in those days not to follow the growing up of illegitimate offspring. At least, there is no record of Francisca claiming, when Francisco, El Marques, became conqueror of the Incas, "That is my son!"

Actually, Francisco was a foundling, having been abandoned just after his birth in 1471, placed outside the door of a church, where he was found and cared for by a compassionate stranger. Subsequently, his father acknowledged him but declined education or normal advantages. Gonzalo was a captain in the Spanish army. Following a military career was a type of social security—steady income just above the poverty level. Perhaps he couldn't afford schooling for his kids or perhaps he preferred to spend his wages on mistresses.

Estremadura should have been a fine place for growing up, with large forests in the North, great for hiking and exploring. There was farming and mining in the South where one could enjoy rural life and learn about coal, copper, and silver. But the Pizarro boys preferred village life in Trujillo, though they were unaware of its beauty with its whitewashed buildings and red tile roofs. Had there been street gangs, they would have been leaders. Had there been graffiti, they would have written obscene messages on those blank walls—all except Francisco who never learned to read or write. Merely writing "X" on a wall wouldn't mean anything.

Those kids learned to fend for themselves. Early on they mastered self-defense with knife and knee. They knew about garroting, a quick way to eliminate an adversary, particularly if you had him outnumbered. They learned not to show fear despite the odds—better to intimidate the other guy with bravado and arrogance. They had no respect for others—a "hooray for me, to hell with you" attitude. They looked forward to serving in the army, for it would provide sword, lance, armor, and training for conquests. They also looked forward to being old enough to engage in a little hanky-panky like their father had.

"Say, monkeyface, let's go down to the barracks and shoot craps with the soldiers. We might pick up some gossip." Francisco was talking to his older brother. "Anyhow, I'd like to talk to Corporal Enrique and find out how he got that scar on his face."

"Can't, Francisco. I promised Juan I'd go to church with him. We're having communion today. Why don't you come along?"

"Me? I go just often enough to have the priest think I'm a good Catholic. No thanks. I'll go down to the barracks by myself."

Despite their bold demeanor, the Pizarro boys were really no different than their contemporaries. They were devout sons of the Church, outwardly, at least.

There was no embarrassment or jealousy among the half-brothers as to their blood and legal relationships. The only value of legitimacy was inheritance and this made little difference, as their father would have very little to leave to his sons.

"Father, the Leon family can't take care of me any longer. The señora has the wobbles. I have no place to go. Can you help me?" Captain Pizarro thought for a minute and said, "Well, Francisco, Carlos down at the farm is getting too blind to keep an eye on the pigs. Why don't you go down there and take over? His old woman can feed you."

"But, Dad, I'm not that desperate."

"Better do as I say, Son. You'll be glad you did. But be sure to keep a close eye on those pigs when they're out in the field. If one gets away I'll tear you apart."

So Francisco became a swineherd, much to his disgust. But his new career didn't last long, for the pigs did escape and he didn't dare tell his father. On sudden impulse he ran away to fend for himself.

Francisco did not know that another handsome youngster, almost the same age, was growing up in Jerez, a hundred miles away: Vasco Núñes de Balboa. They would meet later and each would contribute amazing chapters to world history.

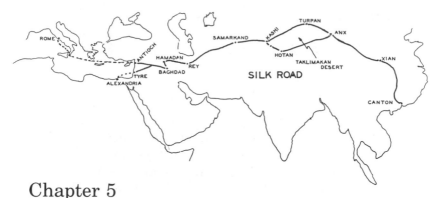

Map labels: ROME, SAMARKAND, TURPAN, ANX, ANTIOCH, HAMADAN, KASHI, HOTAN, XIAN, REY, TAKLIMAKAN DESERT, TYRE, BAGHDAD, SILK ROAD, ALEXANDRIA, CANTON

Chapter 5
Silk and Trade

The Chinese "discovered" silk. Very clever, the Chinese. They not only studied the silkworm and its cocoon but learned to unwind the quarter-mile or so of fiber, then twist several fibers together to make thread, then weave the thread into fabrics. They developed dyeing and the making of exotic garments. They kept their know-how a secret for two thousand years. This added a valuable commodity to their already established trade with European countries. For at least four thousand years their advanced civilization had maintained communication with the Mediterranean area. They traded spices, perfumes, tea, glassware, metalwork, jade, and silks. They also developed a substantial market for horses, those marvelous animals from the Mongolian steppe. All these items were in demand in Europe. Spices, for instance, were indispensable for flavorings and as a food preservative. Silk garments were ever so much more exotic than cottons or woolens.

It is one thing for a venturesome explorer to find a

19

way through unknown territory; quite another for regular caravans. The rigors of travel were formidable. The Taklamakan Desert was six hundred miles wide, with no water, only at widely spaced oases. Windstorms and blowing sand obliterated vision and erased the trail. Under those circumstances a caravan might lose all sense of direction and wander in a circle, to ultimate death. The Karakoram Pass was eighteen thousand feet, nearly the altitude where modern climbers use oxygen. Forage for their two-humped Bactrian camels was meager, if any, but fortunately those durable beasts did well with shortages of food and water and even in sandstorms, being able to close their nostrils. They had a keen sense of direction, especially in "smelling" water and hurrying toward a yet to be seen oasis. As a further safeguard in a sandstorm, the Bactrian camel has an extra membrane to wipe sand off the eyes. As if the tortures of nature were not enough, marauders began menacing the caravans, first begging and later becoming bolder, engaging in armed robbery.

Despite such a discouraging route, trade prospered. Some twelve caravans per year ventured forth—up to a hundred persons with fully loaded camels. A round trip might require as much as eight or nine years. The Chinese terminal cities of Ch'ang-an and later Xian became the most important cities in the world. They found need for military defense. The former is the site of the famous terra-cotta warriors representing the then emperor's army, an enlarged bodyguard. These cities had populations of some two million people. The great Chinese wall was built for defense.

Horses were in demand in India, Spain, and almost everywhere else. Though not as suitable as camels for Silk Road caravans, they became indispensable for both pleasure and work. A maharaja might value his horse more than his family. A villager might make his living through the work of one horse. A Chinese emperor learned that horses vastly superior to the Mongolians' were to be had in the West. These, according to legend, were heaven-sent creatures that sweated blood. He imported some, equipped his cavalry, repelled the Huns, and safeguarded the Silk Road.

Some two hundred years before Columbus, the Polos traveled the Silk Road. They, father and son, were traders. Marco, the son, recorded their saga—and what a story it was! They had accompanied officials in a caravan along the Silk Road. They saw sights that excited every reader of Marco's chronicle, though many deemed it more fiction than fact until it was proven true. The description of the emperor's palace in Cipangu with its gold roof and gold window-frames inspired many. And his observation that Cipangu was some fifteen hundred miles off the coast of China was a telling encouragement to Columbus.

India and Ceylon (Sri Lanka) developed competition in the spices and silks trade and found alternate routes to the Silk Road. Those countries were also more businesslike in their dealings. Whereas the Chinese, in their earlier days at least, had the attitude of bringing gifts and expecting gifts in return, the Indians demanded payment in gold coins. Coins had a prescribed gold content and were thus not subject to adulteration.

The demand for spices and silks was so great that Europe suffered a shortage of gold coins. This is one reason for the intense thirst for gold at the time of Columbus. It also stimulated a resourceful practice: kidnap a maharaja and hold him for ransom payable in gold coins!

Silk became a status symbol. No lady would dare be

seen at a ball unless she wore a silk dress. There is a tale of a beautiful damsel who arrived at a special occasion wearing nothing but a gossamer silk gown! She was a sensation.

Gradually, those alternate routes—some by land and some by sea—were established. Cities like Susa, Persepolis, and Petra became well-known to traders. Gradually, also, the original Silk Road became more hazardous because of marauders. The original route of those brave Chinese merchants and of Alexander the Great and Marco Polo was superseded.

Chapter 6

Japan Ho!

"Admiral, sir, are you awake? May I come in? I saw your light and hoped you might not be asleep." It was the voice of Juan de la Cosa, master and owner of the *Santa Maria* and a close friend of Columbus. As master, he was second in command. Columbus was captain of the *Santa Maria*, captain general of the fleet, and admiral of the Ocean Sea as granted by the queen. "A few minutes ago I was saying my prayers, begging God to calm down the men. The more I thought about their agitation, I realized that I should discuss my worries with you. I fear we may have a mutiny."

"Sit down, Juan. I, too, am concerned, for I have seen the hostile looks on their faces. Who do you think is fomenting trouble?"

"No one in particular, sir, though some of those criminals are real troublemakers. There seems to be a general feeling that we have been away from Palos much too long. Remember what we told them when they enlisted? Here it is October ninth and we have been underway for a month. We have come so far that the helmsman thinks we may have overshot Cipangu. There is fear that we may run out of provisions. The sentiment is that we should reverse direction and go back empty-handed. If not, there is talk of throwing the admiral overboard and claiming it was an accident."

"This worries me, Juan, but I am also determined to reach my goal. The fact that the wind has almost faded away leaves the men with little to do except grumble. They haven't stopped to think about the terrible consequences of arriving back in Palos without having gone those extra few leagues to Cipangu. See that scroll over there? It is Queen Isabella's message to the Grand Khan. I intend to deliver it. And I am sure we will make landfall within a very few days. I'll talk to the men in the morning and tell them so. I'll also tell them that if we don't, I'll be willing to turn back. But between us, Juan, I'll never turn back until after we have landed. There is evidence we are getting close—floating debris, flights of birds, and an occasional swell that is not what you would expect in the middle of a sea, far from land. And my journal confirms this."

Columbus kept two journals—the honest one, which he kept carefully concealed, and another one, which could be seen by his officers and showed lesser distances. He didn't want to reveal just how far they were from home port.

Then, as Columbus was dozing, his mind played back his vivid memory of the past several hectic months. Chartering the *Niña, Pinta,* and *Santa Maria* had been no problem, thanks to the help of his friend, de la Cosa. Well, he did have an argument over naming the flagship. The original name was *Marigalante* (Frivolous Mary), which offended him. They settled on naming it the *Santa Maria*. Recruiting nearly a hundred men for the crews took time, as there were few volunteers. With crown approval he emptied the jails. What with four murderers and other criminals, none of whom were experienced sailors, he incurred a serious risk of trouble. He also cheated a bit on the minimum ages of the gromets (ship's boys). Provisioning was a normal operation, as the skippers and stewards were experienced and funds were at hand. So, after four months of make-ready, August 3, 1492, was set as the date of departure. Columbus said good-bye to his son Ferdinand and made his obeisances at Saint George's. All hands took communion. The port of Palos was crowded, as this was the final departure date for Jews. Finding a breeze, they hoisted sail and headed for the Canaries some six hundred miles away and 150 miles off the coast of Africa. Thus, the motley crews had their first experience of being out of sight of land. From there they would take a westerly course out into the Ocean Sea.

The story of their landfall on October 12, 1492, is so well-known that it need not be repeated here. It, the discovery of America, is on a parallel with the greatest events of all history—thanks to Christopher Columbus.

What is not generally appreciated is that that is not what Columbus had in mind. His objective was, and had been for seven years, to pioneer a sea route to the Indies. Convinced that he had arrived there, he called the natives Indians and, though it is hard to understand why, the name stuck. That scroll addressed to the Grand Khan of Japan was written in Arabic in belief that all peoples of like latitude spoke that language. He even brought along an interpreter, Luis de Torres, who knew Hebrew and some Arabic. The greeting was never delivered. Columbus didn't even name America. That was done inadvertently through a signature by Amerigo Vespucci, a chartmaker and adventurer, on his chart of the newly found Western World. The name seemed appropriate and caught hold—much better than "Vespucciland" or some other term. But too bad it wasn't a name related to the discoverer.

Lest lighthearted tales of Columbus create a feeling that he was inept, let's look at the record:

He was a superb navigator, using skills acquired through studying expert contemporaries and perfecting them through years of trial and error. His navigational aids were few. First, a magnetic compass. He didn't know, though, of magnetic variation due to the geographic North Pole and magnetic North Pole being in two different places. He used a knotted line for measuring speed and distance, with knots spaced equally. The end of the line had a "log" which held still in the water. The line was paid out and the number of knots (hence the term) pulled over the transom were counted while the half-hour glass measured time. A half-hour glass was also tended by the watch who turned it over the instant the sand ran through. He then rang the ship's bell, once for each half hour elapsed since he came on duty. The length of a watch was four hours or eight bells.

He had a marine quadrant for making solar observations to determine latitude, but didn't have much faith in it. It was a quarter-circle of hardwood, the circular edge of which had ninety-degree marks. The straight edge nearest the ninety-degree mark had two brackets with sighting holes. From the apex, a plumb bob was suspended on a silk cord. The observer held the contraption vertically so that the cord laid against the degree marks. Then, by sighting through the peep holes and sighting at the North Star, the observer would call "mark." The accomplice would read the number of degrees where the cord intersected. This was the latitude. The reading was reasonably accurate so long as the night was clear and the ship wasn't rolling or pitching or yawing too much, and they weren't too close to the equator where Polaris was near the horizon and obscured by sea-level atmosphere and haze.

How about longitude? The most accurate determinant in the age of Columbus was a total eclipse! Early astronomers had studied those phemomena to the extent that they could predict them. They published tables that, for Columbus, provided data for eclipses in 1494 and 1503—of no use on that first voyage. But the table advised that one should note the time of the eclipse, note the time shown for the astronomer's reference and figure the difference in hours and fractions—then multiply it by fifteen to convert it to degrees (the earth: 360 degrees; full day: 24 hours). Anyhow, Marco Polo hadn't provided the longitude of Cipangu for comparison. So Columbus was stymied on longitude. Many other mariners were, too. There had been no agreement on a prime meridian. Astronomers tended to place it on their home cities. Once, there was agreement on having it west of the Canaries, probably feeling that Europe could thus be East and the western world West Longitude. Then British astronomers made a case for a prime meridian passing through the Royal Observatory at Greenwich. It was adopted internationally, but not until late 1884!

Today we are most fortunate. For less than three hundred dollars you can buy a small electronic device that will "talk" to a satellite and tell you your position, within a few feet, any place in the world.

After his landfall, Columbus explored through the Caribbean islands, very carefully, to avoid shoals or getting becalmed. He named islands for Isabella and Ferdinand. Coming to Cuba, he thought it was the mainland. Seeing no Chinese junks and only scanty evidence of humans, he sent a party inland to search for evidence of the Grand Khan's palace and for evidence of gold. Some naked natives wore a bit of gold and pointed in the direction of its source.

Cuba had something else new to the Spaniards: tobacco. The natives grew the plant, dried the mature leaves, rolled them into a "cigar," inserted it into a nostril, lighted it, and inhaled. That tobacco started a revolution is an understatement. Once it was introduced into Europe the demand for cigars, snuff, and pipe tobacco soon supported a major industry. Columbus, who had bargained at length for a portion of any riches, failed to recognize any commercial value.

Meanwhile Columbus made a stab at figuring his latitude. He sighted on the wrong star which showed him too far north. For longitude he added the notations from his secret journal. Thus he convinced himself that he had missed Japan and was on the coast of Asia.

After some more exploring, they picked up some natives to train as interpreters, acquired some gold, and decided to head for home. There were two compelling questions: how to convince the queen that they had been in the land of Cathay, and how to find their way back to Spain.

En route they made a most fortunate landfall at Haiti, for there was a large colony of natives and an abundance of gold jewelry, which was willingly traded for a few trinkets. All went well until the *Santa Maria* grounded on a coral reef the night before Christmas. Christmas day was spent salvaging cargo with the help of natives with dugout canoes. A hasty settlement, Navidad, was established and a colony of thirty-nine men was left, to be rescued at some future date.

The *Niña* became the new flagship. Both the *Niña* and the *Pinta* were leaking badly, so they were careened and caulked. At long last they ventured into the Ocean Sea.

In three weeks they came to the Azores despite being becalmed in the Sargasso Sea and contending with a violent storm near the Azores. They stopped there to stow wood and water. Taking a chance on the stormy weather, they guessed wrong and sailed right into a major cyclone.

Seeing the tip of Portugal was a tremendous relief. Most sails were torn to shreds and some of the crew had expected to sink. Going up the Tagus River toward Lisbon, they were greeted with awe, then with hostility. Getting out of Portuguese clutches after paying respects to royalty, the Admiral with the two caravels returned to the same Spanish harbor they had left thirty-two weeks previously.

Columbus had already written his report and had begun to plan his next voyage to the West Indies. He learned that the queen and king were in Barcelona, some eight hundred miles away. A messenger was sent on muleback, requesting an audience. The round trip must have taken a month and a half. At last, the reply came and, in effect, said: "Hurry to Barcelona. We are delighted." So the admiral with his naked "Exhibits A" and some gold and a few items such as caged parrots, was welcomed in Barcelona.

Columbus was at the height of his fame. Spain was launched toward world prominence.

Chapter 7

Portugal Lays Claim

No sooner had Columbus returned to Spain than the Portuguese asserted claim to the newly discovered lands. They had documentary substantiation as a result of their explorations along the west coast of Africa, around the Cape of Good Hope, and partway up the East Coast. A treaty had been drawn, giving Portugal exclusive rights to all lands she should discover in Guinea and off the coast of it, except the Canaries. Ferdinand and Isabella had signed it. Pope Sixtus IV had confirmed it in 1481.

It should be understood that, by common understanding among kingdoms, the territorial claims of discoverers of lands "not already under the rule of a Christian Prince" were respected. And the Pope made final decisions.

The Spanish king and queen learned that the Portuguese were already assembling a fleet to visit the new world. They were consternated. Something had to be done to correct the situation. And this had to involve the Pope. By this time the Pope was Alexander VI, a Borgia, who was beholden to the Spanish sovereigns in more ways than one. So, they drafted a proposed Bull and forwarded it. It was promptly approved, giving Spain all new lands in the West, toward the Indies, including any yet to be discovered! There went the entire Western Hemisphere!

The Portuguese objected and, on second thought, so did the Spanish, for they had decided to seek dominion of the sea itself. Columbus had been consulted and had proposed a demarcation line. There was so much arguing and bickering that Columbus had departed on his second voyage when both parties decided to arbitrate. The result was a treaty signed on June 7, 1494, in Tordesillas, Spain. It established a line of demarcation on a north-south meridian 370 leagues west of the Cape Verde Islands. Everything west of it went to Spain, and everything east to Portugal. It is now recognized as Longitude 46° 30′ West.

Thus, by treaty and not by Papal decree, the two kingdoms resolved their argument, not knowing what the future held for them. Portugal would discover later that the line hits the coast of South America near the mouth of the Amazon, thus giving them title to Brazil—where Portuguese became, as it still is, the official language.

By looking west rather than east, the Portuguese didn't realize that the Philippine Islands were more east than west of the Tordesillas meridian. Spain claimed the Philippines, and Spanish became the official language. But the Portuguese, having taken a quick look at Brazil, didn't feel that it had a great potential. Instead, their top priority became the pioneering of a sea route to the lands of spices and silks.

The Treaty of Tordesillas is one of the greatest successes in the history of understandings among nations. Despite their rivalry, and the heavy-handedness of early explorers and colonizers, both sides honored and respected it.

Chapter 8
Voyages 2, 3, and 4

After his great discovery Columbus still had a lot of unfinished business. He hadn't found a major source of gold. He couldn't yet prove that he had come to the Asiatic mainland. He had yet to Christianize the natives. He wanted to colonize the new lands with Spanish settlers. He wanted to fulfill the expectations of his adored queen. And above all, he was impelled by his own stubbornness and sense of purpose to keep going.

Thus he had drafted his proposal for a second voyage before the first one was completed. The sovereigns not only approved—they urged him to hasten. So, within five months a fleet of seventeen vessels was assembled, some chartered, some purchased. Over twelve hundred men (no women) were recruited to fill a list of required skills—farmers, miners, mechanics, soldiers, and priests. This was to be the largest colonization effort in Spanish history.

Voyage 2

After stopping at the Canaries they sighted land at Dominica, then went on to San Juan Bautista (Puerto Rico) where an encouraging source of gold dust and nuggets was located. A devastating illness overtook more than a third of the party. So, five months after leaving Spain, twelve of the fifteen ships headed for home for the sick to get well. One can only conjecture why so many suddenly decided to abandon their great opportunity: "This land is unhealthy. Why didn't someone tell us?" "The natives don't look like they want us around. Well, I don't like them either." "Somehow I thought we would come to a golden land like the Garden of Eden. I didn't think we'd have to work to get rich. Work? I'm not for it." "Colonize? No. I just want to become rich and hurry home to spend it." So off they went and took with them ample evidence of the resources of the new lands—gold, spices, parrots, two dozen natives, and letters to the sovereigns. The letters requested several vessels to hurry back with provisions, clothing, work animals, and medical supplies.

The queen and king, surprisingly, were still supportive. Everything that Columbus requested was approved. Meanwhile Columbus and company went on and came to a land so sizable that they thought it was a mainland. It was Cuba. They also chose a site for a fort and established it with fifty men, some horses, agricultural tools, etc. In honor of their queen it was named Isabella. After four months of exploring the coastline they decided it was a peninsula of the mainland. Returning to the Isabella settlement they were surprised to see the caravels that they had requested, under the command of brother Bartholomew whom Christopher hadn't seen in several years. Now they had provisions and reinforcements.

Friar Pane had finally baptized the first native, then returned to Spain full of venom against the Columbus brothers, telling of cruelty to the natives and disaffection of the colonists. An investigating officer arrived, full of prejudice. Columbus felt he must return to Spain to straighten out the situation. En route he was becalmed again. His party went ashore at Guadaloupe Island where they were ambushed but managed to take on wood, water, and some foodstuffs. They struggled into Cadiz half-starved and bedraggled.

So Voyage 2 was no breakthrough. Columbus had had enough adversity to convince any normal person to give up. Gossip had spread to the point that he was jeered in public. He had developed arthritis and was beginning to feel like an old man. To be less conspicuous he adopted the brown habit of a Franciscan. He lived in monasteries. The queen and king learned of his hardships and invited him to come see them. He did. And guess what—he proposed a third voyage! Even more surprising—Their Majesties approved it!

Voyage 3

This time there was less urgency. Two years were spent assembling a fleet of eight ships, crews, provisions, and three hundred colonizers at state expense, plus an additional fifty who might go at their own expense. Women's Lib had a first: one woman per ten men. The

34

jails must have filled again, for convicted murderers, arsonists, counterfeiters, and sodomists were eligible. Their sentences were commuted, required lengths of stay proportionate to the severity of their sentences. Getting equipped and under way was chaotic. By late 1498 they hoisted sails, with Columbus in poor condition, both mentally and physically.

It was deemed important to find out whether there was land on the Portuguese side of the Tordesillas meridian, so they steered a southerly course, taking on wood and water at Madeira, then on to the Cape Verde islands. Some sixty days later, having been becalmed again in tropical heat, they made a landfall at Trinidad, just in time, for their perishables had spoiled and their water was almost gone. They came to an abundance of water at a river mouth where everyone bathed, swam and laundered. Too bad they didn't realize that that much water had to flow from a continent. It was the Orinoco River. Too bad, also, that they didn't know that teredos (ship worms) can't survive in fresh water. Anchoring there a week or two would have cleaned the planking better than careening and applying tar.

They went on to the tip of the Paria Peninsula of Venezuela, still not recognizing the land as part of a continent. Nor was any mention made as to which side of the Tordesillas meridian they were. But they did appreciate coming to some peaceful natives who excelled in weaving and jewelry made from a gold-copper alloy. They had beautiful pearls and made necklaces of alternate seeds and pearls that would sell well today. But the Spaniards failed to learn that marvelous pearl beds were nearby.

From there they went on to the settlement at Santo Domingo. Despite the circuitous approach, Columbus was right on target. Those at the settlement were glad to see them, though the settlement had really gone downhill. Natives had been maltreated. Some colonists had contracted syphilis. Ex-criminals had commandeered caravels. Other colonists had rebelled. The colony had become completely uncivilized. Unfortunately, Christopher's son Don Diego who never should have been given that kind of responsibility, was in charge.

Word about all this, blaming the Columbus brothers, had reached the sovereigns. Becoming wary, they sent a trusted leader, Bobadilla, as Chief Justice to straighten out the grievances. His arrival had preceded Christopher's and he was already prejudiced.

When Christopher arrived he, without a hearing, was arrested, placed in chains and sent to Spain. En route the captain offered to remove the chains but stubborn Christopher refused, saying that since Their Majesties had ordered his arrest, only they could order them removed.

On his arrival in Spain the prisoner and his jailer went to a monastery. A pathetic letter was forwarded to the queen who was residing in the Alhambra in Granada. In due time Christopher was summoned, released from chains, and his rights and income were restored. But by this time it was realized that he lacked ability as a ruler. His governance was not re-established. And his request for punishment of Chief Justice Bobadilla, because of his precipitous arrest, was not heeded.

The urge to colonize the New World continued. One Ovando was named Governor. He sailed with thirty vessels and a complement of twenty-five hundred crew and colonists. And Columbus, down but far from out, decided to ask for support of a fourth voyage!

Voyage 4

Their Highnesses approved Voyage 4 on March 14, 1502. It was hoped that Columbus might find a strait providing access to Asia, permitting him to circumnavigate the world. Perhaps this voyage would be his crowning glory. Undoubtedly it would be his last, for at age fifty-one he was an old man by maritime standards.

This time the fleet was four caravels with 135 men and boys. The ships were carefully selected for seaworthiness. Christopher named a younger man captain of the flagship. Brother Bartholomew and son Ferdinand went along on separate ships.

This time they departed without fanfare. From Seville to Cadiz they awaited favorable weather; then they put to sea for the Canaries, where they would take on the usual wood and water. From there they made the Atlantic crossing in three weeks, to Martinique. Thence to Dominica where they sought refuge from a forthcoming hurricane. Columbus knew his weather and his arthritis gave him extra warning. They requested entry into the harbor and learned that a fleet of thirty ships was about to sail for Spain. Columbus quickly warned that the fleet should delay until the hurricane had passed. The prejudiced governor refused entry and ordered the fleet to depart. Came disaster. Only one of the thirty ships survived and more than five hundred lives were lost. Columbus meanwhile had found shelter downcoast.

With the weather improved, the four caravels headed for the coast of Central America. There they suffered incessant rain. At one point they entered a channel which they hoped might be that long sought strait. No luck. But

Columbus did learn that he was close to another ocean, nine days' march away. Deducing that he was on a peninsula, he needed the search for a strait and turned his attention to finding gold. Farther along the coast they came to a beautiful harbor which they called Porto Bello, then went eastward and founded Nombre de Dios. Weather! Weather! Weather!

One caravel entered the mouth of the Rio Belen, crossing the bar at about seven feet depth. Then the weather improved, the river dropped and the ship was trapped. Nothing to do but pray for more rain to raise the river level—and spend the time searching for gold. The natives had been friendly and helpful but when they felt that the Spanish were there to stay, they attacked with poisoned arrows. The trapped party made a sort of catamaran with two canoes and escaped to the ships anchored offshore. In the fracas they lost ten men, the caravel and its small boat. Columbus meanwhile had incurred malaria.

Abandoning the Isthmus, the three ships followed the coast until they could take a tack for Hispaniola. They soon learned that while they had been at anchor teredos had been boring vigorously. The hulls began leaking like sieves. One ship was abandoned. The remaining two limped through terrible weather to the Cuban coast, pumping and bailing all the way. Half sunk, out of rations, the situation was foreboding. Thanks to the admiral's ability at dead reckoning and his determination under stress, they ran downwind to Jamaica, and found dry harbor on the north shore. No water. No supplies. So, on another two hours or so to Puerto Santa Gloria which Columbus had named seven years before. Unable to keep the two caravels afloat any longer they beached them. No other ship could be expected to call there, nor could they sail on. What to do? Find some natives, "buy" some food, for they were starving. Then, if possible, get a dugout canoe to attempt a crossing to the settlement at Hispaniola. Only a hundred miles or so of open sea! This is exactly what they did.

They acquired a canoe and a crew of six "Indians." Diego Mendez volunteered to go seek help and carry a message to be forwarded to the queen. The canoe was fitted with raised washboards, a mast, and a sail. The first leg of the trip was downcoast, where further progress was frustrated by hostile natives. Mendez returned. An additional canoe was recruited and another Spaniard volunteered to lead. This time each canoe took six Spaniards and ten "Indians," hoping that at least one might make it. Tears were shed as the two canoes departed, then stifled for a long, long wait.

For the canoers the heat was unbearable. The natives jumped overboard, one at a time, to cool off. Thirst overtook all. In three days they made a landfall—right at forbidding rocky cliffs. But there they found some water in depressions. Mendez helped gather shellfish. Refreshed, they paddled the final thirty miles during the night. Governor Ovando, the one who refused Columbus's entry previously, was nonplussed. Humanity vs. sentiment. Humanity won.

Meanwhile, the Spaniards back at Santa Gloria mutinied. Some tried to escape and failed. The natives became hostile. Columbus tried a form of sorcery to gain their sympathy. He had kept his solar ephemerus which predicted a lunar eclipse. He assembled the chiefs, told them the moon would soon darken if they wouldn't become friends. They were overawed and offered their respect. This was also a means of determining longitude but this was a futile gesture.

After a seemingly interminable wait a rescue ship arrived—eight months after the canoes had departed. The group was taken back to Santo Domingo and were transferred to a ship going to Spain. By this time Columbus was broken in health and spirit. His son Ferdinand was now sixteen, having lived a lifetime, experiencewise.

The queen had earlier received the admiral's message. She had been startled and offended. Columbus, on arrival in Spain, was fifty-three, old, fragile, and grumpy. The queen ignored him. The Fourth voyage had been in vain—or had it? When, in all history, has there been such a record of determination and resourcefulness in surviving under extremely adverse conditions?

The queen became ill and soon thereafter died. Columbus had lost his foremost advocate. His income continued. He had servants and attendants. Yet he, stubborn, continued to complain about injustices.

The king refused to see him. But his son Don Diego had won the king's admiration and became a member of the Royal Guard. He later was appointed Governor of Hispaniola. (He had married Dona Marie de Toledo, the king's cousin, which helped.)

Nearing his end, Christopher named Don Diego as heir and wrote his last will and testament. Last rites were timely, as he died May 20, 1506.

What can we make of all this? Superb navigational ability? Yes. Conviction that Cipangu was accessible to the West? Definitely yes. Dedication throughout his life to a single purpose? Yes. Ability to survive despite the most devastating of events? Yes! Ability to govern? No. We will long revere Christopher Columbus for all that he achieved. For his shortcomings, well, we all have blind sides and so must forgive them.

Here's to Christopher Columbus, one of the most deserving heroes in all history!

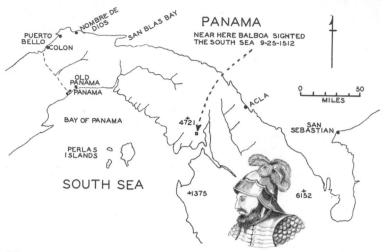

Chapter 9
To The Pacific

I learned in the fourth grade that Balboa discovered the Pacific. I had visions of a handsome young Spanish officer wearing armor and helmet standing atop a bare, round-topped hill, extending his right arm and pointing to a never-before-seen sea, the Pacific. The air was crystal-clear and the weather was cool. Well, all this was as far from the truth as Japan was from where Columbus thought it was. But history does record correctly that Vasco Núñez de Balboa saw the Pacific on September 26, 1513. He called it the South Sea, for the isthmus runs east-west and the Pacific is to the south. With Balboa was Francisco Pizarro about whom we shall have much more to say.

The Panamanian isthmus was nearly impenetrable

jungle, inhabited by scattered colonies of natives who were hostile to each other and to any intruder. Exploring inland, Balboa and company suffered some losses but managed to appease the natives with trinkets and small bells. They found the women very accommodating. They acquired a few gold artifacts and gestured that they were seeking more. The natives were perceptive enough to realize that armed resistance was futile, that the Spaniards wanted gold more than anything else, and that life would be better if they would just go. So they told the Spaniards that gold was farther on, lots of it.

Balboa and his party, what was left of it, returned to the Caribbean side to confer with others. How to get ships into the South Sea? The decision resulted in one of the most stupendous undertakings ever—to build ships on the Pacific side and sail them for that promised gold. No more mention of sailing westward for spices and other treasures. Gold was now their objective. Now, how to go about building ships? Just copy one of the brigantines, fabricate its elements, piece by piece, portage them across the isthmus, and assemble them on the Pacific shore!

The next ship back to Spain bore a requisition for shipbuilders and parts such as ship's bells, pulleys, and anchors, for four brigantines. A new settlement was founded and named Acla, some three hundred miles downcoast from Porto Bello, at the narrowest part of the isthmus. The river there might be suitable for barging. Trees were felled, beautiful hardwoods, finer than the oaks of Spain that were becoming scarce. Huge tree trunks were hewed for keels. Gradually, ship's knees, ribs, strakes, planking, and decking took shape. Then came the almost insurmountable task—transportation.

There was no trail. The jungle was so dense that no sunlight reached the ground. Vines and air plants were interwoven, providing a habitat for noisy birds and poisonous snakes, spiders, and tarantulas. Wild animals begrudgingly yielded, and an occasional ocelot gave up reluctantly. One had to beware of vampire bats and scorpions. The temperature was unbearably hot, day and night. The humidity seemed total, which it was much of the time, in the form of rain. Screeching monkeys competed with swarms of cicadas for incessant din. blocking out human speech and even thought. And there were mosquitoes, mosquitoes, mosquitoes. Hacking through was ever so slow. Some days they progressed only a few feet and weren't sure they were going in the right direction.

Men developed fever and after a few days died. The air was blamed, probably because it had the odor of decaying things. In Spanish it was "mal aire," anglicized as *malaria*. Four hundred years later it was learned that malaria is transmitted by the anopheles mosquito, one that appears to be standing on its head when it bites.

The loss of life was prodigious, but the men persisted and finally stacked their weird cargo on the shore of the Pacific. The party of 780 men was now 60. Alonzo Martín de Don Benito was one who survived. He had carried one of the anchors across the isthmus.

Came the task of assembling the brigantines. Still alive were men of experience who selected sites for ways and laid two keels on log rollers. The other two keels would wait and, in fact, were never used. Finally, the carpenters could lay down their tools. The masts were hoisted into their sockets, rigging and sails installed. Someone rang a ship's bell amidst great hilarity on June 24, 1518, five years after the discovery of the Pacific.

Our friend Balboa assumed the honor of commanding one of the brigantines on its shakedown cruise—the first European ship to sail on the Pacific. On the shakedown he discovered the Pearl Islands and returned with unexpected treasure, marvelous pearls almost as valuable as gold. What a gift for Queen Isabella! She would be delighted.

Balboa, despite his firsts and unusual talent, had a tragic end. In appreciation of his efforts, the governor, Pedrarias Davila, had arranged for his daughter to come to the New World to become Balboa's bride. Jealousy developed and Balboa was double-crossed, falsely accused of misappropriation, arrested, given a summary trial, and executed by garroting. In retrospect, this dastardly deed denied the New World a brilliant leader who knew how make friends with the natives, inspire the best efforts of his contemporaries, and deal with his superiors with respect. Pizarro witnessed the execution, presumably without remorse, for he had set his mind on other things—sailing down the Pacific for gold.

Pedrarius continued his tightfisted regime. But instead of following leads to find gold to the south, he engaged in several expeditions to the north, venturing into what is now Costa Rica, Nicaragua, and Honduras.

Chapter 10

The Pre-Incas

Now that we are acquainted with the remarkable achievements of the Incas and their predecessors it is only fair to ask: Where did they come from and how did they get here? There are at least two schools of thought, and it is worth our while to study both. Let's go back twenty-five or thirty thousand years and search for evidence.

First, we must rule out the possibility of their originating right in South America. There is absolutely no evidence that this could have occurred, though Pope Julius II in 1512 thought he settled the matter when he pronounced that the "Indians" were descended from Adam and Eve. Then we must discard any thought that these people came from the Nile, despite the fact that the two cultures had much in common. The learned community did not stick with Fray Gregorio García who published a book in 1607 stating that some were probably

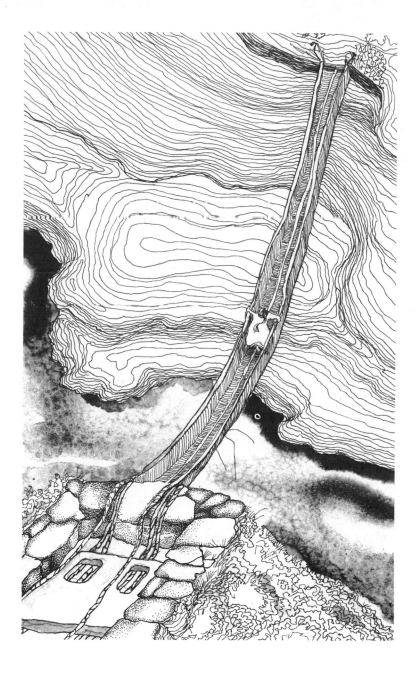

descended from the Carthaginians, others from the Lost Tribes, some from the lost continent of Atlantis, Phoenicians, and more than a thousand Chinese, Tartar, and other groups!

For many years the sole theory of archaeologists and anthropologists was that early man in the Americas came from Asia on a land bridge which crossed the sea during the Great Ice Age when much of the earth's water was locked up in polar ice caps and the sea level was a hundred feet or more below the present level. Yes, there is evidence to support this theory and it has been universally accepted.

For early man, survival must have been his paramount concern, meaning, first, food—following edible animals and finding vegetable foods. Once over the land bridge game would have been more plentiful in warmer climes, thus leading him south. Of equal importance would have been the perpetuation of the species, so it is axiomatic that women came along and probably did some of the stalking and hunting. High on the list of priorities would have been adaptability. It is hard to imagine how humans in a relatively short period of time here could have developed such a wide diversity of mannerisms and physical characteristics—or did some arrive with differences? California alone had more than sixty tribes with differing facial features and customs. In the United States there are some six hundred Indian languages and, throughout history, more than a thousand. Add Canada, Mexico, Central America, and South America, and the total is staggering. Migrations did go all the way to Tierra del Fuego, some twelve thousand miles from the Bering Strait—and early man must have meandered and tarried in getting there.

A recent study of genes indicates that all of the natives in the Western Hemisphere were descended from a small band of "pioneers" that included perhaps as few as four women. Startling! Additional research is under way. Perhaps the study was confined to too few samples.

So long as there was adequate food and reasonable comfort, there wasn't really any reason to migrate farther. So, advancing to the south must have been very, very slow. There might have been reasons for moving camp once in a while because it became too cluttered with debris or unbearable with odors. Laplanders do. Or they might have followed the seasonal migrations of animals. Natives in the Serengeti do. In any event, some quarries of obsidian or quartz used in weapon- and tool making were used for centuries, indicating that some settlements were relatively static. Those who lived along the shore may have crafted boats or rafts which could speed their migration.

Recognizing that the isthmus of Panama and northern Venezuela/Colombia cannot be traversed except with extreme difficulty, it seems most likely that travel past those areas had to be by sea. The sparse population inland is another clue that earliest man didn't tarry here. In the late 1400s the Spanish tried to penetrate those jungles and gave up in frustration. When Balboa got to the Pacific he found that traffic was by sea.

Early anthropologists conjectured that the source of the migrants was Central Asia. The theory was widely accepted. Later, studies of physical characteristics led to a belief that earliest man in the Americas must have come from Polynesia. Knowing that the Polynesians were adventurous seafarers, studies centered on possible links.

It seemed possible that the Polynesians might have negotiated the five or six thousand miles across the Pacific to Easter Island or possibly directly to South

America. Even so, they did not rule out the Bering Strait theory. Perhaps there was more than one means of access.

Then came another theory by those who studied ocean currents and prevailing winds. In the northern hemisphere currents are primarily clockwise, going north up the coast of Asia, east below the Aleutians and south along the North American coast, at velocities up to four or five miles per hour. Could earliest man have sailed thus, either willfully or inadvertently? Could this have been a migratory route for the Polynesians?

In the southern hemisphere the currents are primarily counterclockwise—up the coast of South America and west below the equator. Could earliest man have gone from Peru to Easter Island or to the South Pacific Islands or both? Scientists like Harold Gladwin and Thor Heyerdahl have been searching for substantiating evidence.

The pre-Incas developed reed boats on Lake Titicaca and balsa rafts on the Pacific Coast. Heyerdahl reproduced a reed boat and sailed it across the Pacific showing feasibility and demonstrating that a reed boat could remain at sea for a month or so without waterlogging. The ocean current provided much of the propulsion. He also pointed out that whereas land routes left evidence of travel, the seas left no footprints, a feature that deluded most archaeologists. Yet there is a bit of evidence. Chinese vessels are known to have reached the California coast some three thousand years ago by way of the "Black Stream," traveling as much as seventy-five to a hundred miles per day. Chinese coins and an ivory fan are among artifacts unearthed near Cambria, California. Oriental stone anchors have been retrieved in several places.

Heyerdahl concentrated on searching for clues to support his theory that Easter Islanders came from Peru and that pre-Incas came from Polynesia via the North

Pacific. He conducted an extensive study with many excavations on Easter Island. And, as this chapter was being written, was readying a detailed study along the coast of Peru.

Reed boats with unique ends were common to both, as were double-bladed paddles. The pre-Incas quarried massive stones, moved them considerable distances and fitted them together with precision, all without tools as we know them. So did the Easter Islanders. Such work does not occur elsewhere. The statues in the San Agustin area of Colombia have a close resemblance to those on Easter Island. Easter is now denuded of forest cover and is relatively dry. Yet evidence of totora reeds in an ancient swamp have been excavated. They are native in Lake Titicaca where they are used for making reed boats.

Mythical creatures depicted on ceramic vases, such as birdmen, are common to both, though the Islanders carved theirs on stone. The Incas and their predecessors pierced earlobes and inserted decorative or ritualistic objects. These were gradually enlarged. Both had "long ears."

Yet to be explained is the origin of the inventiveness of the pre-Incas and the source of legends like the one about the ancient visitations of bearded white men. The Incas smelted ore, and also made castings with the unique "lost wax" process. They made bronze which can only be produced where there is a source of both copper and tin and the means to melt them. The Egyptians experimented for centuries for a way to harden copper for better weapons and tools. They finally found the right formula. Was the Peruvian equivalent pure coincidence? Or the result of communication? The search for valid answers must continue.

I, for one, go along with the Heyerdahl theory,

namely, that the pre-Incas came from Polynesia by sea, with the aid of ocean currents, north past Japan, easterly below the Aleutians and southerly along the west coast of the Americas. Once established in Inca country they could have, with the boost of westerly currents, gone to, say, Easter Island.

Chapter 11
The Incas

From time to time, with no anticipated outcome, humankind has had bursts of enlightenment. The Greeks with their law and philosophy, the Romans with their technology and governance, the Egyptians with their wisdom, the enduring religions with their moral values, the world's scientists and engineers with their deciphering of the laws of nature and contributions for better living—and the Incas with their several advancements. We could name many more breakthroughs, but for the moment let's talk about the Incas and their unique place in world history.

The origin of the Inca Empire is not known exactly, but is believed to be somewhere around A.D. 1,000. Although it took shape rather quickly, it was preceded by several thousand years of cultural progress, equaling or exceeding that of Europe or Asia. The Europeans and Asians had an advantage—they intercommunicated. An advancement in, say, metallurgy, was soon equaled or exceeded in a neighboring country. The Peruvians did not, for they were isolated from the rest of the world.

Among earlier advancements by the pre-Incas, agriculture and controlled irrigation were well established by 2,500 B.C. The immense alignments in the Nazca Desert date back to 400 B.C. and their neighbors on the Paracas Peninsula excelled in weaving at about the same time. Quarrying and building huge rock structures were well advanced three thousand years ago.

The earliest Inca rulers put several of these advancements together. The originator, Manco Capac, appealed

to the mythological reverence of his subjects, contending that he and his sister arose on the Island of the Sun in Lake Titicaca, offspring of the omnipotent sun. Feeling that the strain should be kept pure, he married his sister and started a custom that persisted generation to generation. The natives respected and revered this supremacy.

The emperor imposed an ironclad authority. He did all the planning for the entire populace. His subjects liked this arrangement, never questioning his authority, seemingly pleased to be relieved of doing their own decision making. They did not realize that they thus became slaves, for they were assured of food and shelter and life's benefits in return for their work at assigned tasks. No payrolls, no money—just enjoyment of a bountiful life. There was, however, an assessor of sorts who knew what was needed by way of food for consumption and storage, and who allotted crop growing. And each wife wove a garment each year, for the government.

The strict regimen included its own form of law and justice. No thievery, as it was punishable by death. No adultery, as it, too, was punishable by death. No stickups, no lawyers, no jails. What a wonderful life! No schools, no teachers, no books, no written language. But kids lived a strict life under the tutelage of parents and the supervision of inspectors.

There were rewards for excellence. The most attractive girls could become virgins in the royal court. The most capable ladies could become members of the royal family. Then there was art. The most talented artisans were shifted from household hobbies to full-time careers in gold working or pottery making. The fleetest youths could become messengers.

Manco Capac professed a mandate to build a huge community center. He built Cuzco, their first city. He felt need for defense against attack by unfriendly tribes and built the then impregnable Sacsahuanan Fortress.

All went reasonably well for several generations. There were conflicts with tribes out on the fringes. There were caprices of weather that either washed out crops or ended in drought. There were acts of the supernatural, like volcanic eruptions, avalanches, and earthquakes. But thanks to the Inca chieftains, they survived and thrived.

Emperor Number eleven, Huayna Capac, died without naming a successor. According to custom, the successor was the most able son of the emperor and his sister-queen. Son Huascar was deemed to be the most able, but there was question as to his lineage. Another son was Atahualpa, one of the many other offspring, who laid claim to the empire. So the empire was divided, half to each. This resulted in dispute and a five-year war. Atahualpa won and started for Cuzco to be proclaimed Emperor of the entire kingdom.

By a unique quirk of history, the fracas occurred just as Francisco Pizarro was nearing Incaland. The timing couldn't have been better for the Spanish.

Chapter 12
Growing up in Inca Country

"Listen, my children. Listen very carefully, because I am about to tell you the story of the Incas. When I have finished, I want each one of you, one at a time, to repeat the story back to me, word for word—exactly as my father told me and his father told him and exactly as you will tell your children some day." Sinche, the father, was speaking. He had a nice fire glowing in the crisp Andes evening. The children were bundled in their warm alpaca robes and were sitting back to back for support, bright-eyed with anticipation. They were already acquainted with the ritual of learning their language and their history step by step—for this episode was only one of many. They were aware that it would be necessary to learn to pronounce and understand every word. But they did not realize that this was because they had no written language, no books, no libraries. The only way their culture could survive was by the process of speaker–listener–speaker.

Sinchi started: "Look in the sky after dawn and honor the Sun God. He marches across the sky every day, keeping an eye on every one of us. Look at his color—gold. He owns all the gold in the world and we take care of it for him. Look at the moon at night—silver. The moon owns all the silver in the world. Don't ever steal gold or silver, else the gods will see and will punish you.

"Once upon a time the Sun God created the first Inca, Manco Capac, and his sister. This was on the Isle of the Sun in the lake which we call Titicaca. They were endowed with great wisdom and the Sun God told them to teach all of our people. He also instructed them to build a beautiful city. They did, and this we call Cuzco.

"The Incas prospered and were great rulers. They taught us to till the soil and grow all the things we eat. They taught us to defend ourselves if an enemy appears. They taught us to build roads for quick access to every ayllu (colony) and like our forebears to build massive stone walls for fortresses and buildings. They taught us to gather gold and silver and make beautiful things. They taught us that we can work hard in high mountains and can run great distances without tiring if we chew the leaf of the coca plant. They taught us to live peacefully with each other. Yes, to the Sun God and the Inca emperors we owe everything we have."

One by one the children repeated the story without error and went off to sleep and to dream of what a wonderful world they lived in.

Babies were not yet part of this custom, but they were the center of household life. As soon as one could stand, he was placed in a baby-size pit that had been dug in the center of activity. Impossible to crawl away. No need for diapers. And no lack of love and attention. Even the guinea pigs that scurried around the yard became friendly, liking the coos and gurgles and attempts to grab them. The babes didn't know that for lunch they were given the broth from guinea pig stew.

As they approached marriageable age, young men and women were expected to get acquainted sexually. Such relationships were not considered promiscuous, though they might involve a number of different partners. It was felt that the finding of companionate compatibility should result in happy marriages. If a marriageable youth was slow in finding a mate, his parents would arrange a marriage. Once one was married, faithfulness was mandatory. Adultery was punishable by death. Sexual activity was not only condoned, it was expected. It inspired a variety of modes and extremes that resulted in diseases which we will discuss later.

One more reference to their language seems appropriate. It was expressive and extensive. Much of it depended on intonation and to this extent it was close to being musical. A slight change in pitch or gutteral sounds could change the meaning. A close parallel was the language of the Tierra del Fuegans, relatives at the southernmost tip of South America. We mention them here because we know more about their speech. When Charles Darwin visited them and saw how primitive they were in appearance, he wrote that they were as close to the missing link as he could imagine. He failed to study their language. Years later a missionary not only learned their language but over a period of thirty years developed a phonetic dictionary, a compilation of more than thirty-two thousand words. He wrote that their language was more expressive than either English or Spanish. For example, where English has one word for ice, the Fuegans had several to describe its condition, where it was found, etc. Relaying their verbal "dictionary" to others didn't seem to be difficult. To us, today, it would seem to be an impossibility.

Children learned chants and songs. It was easy to memorize a chant. And singing the words of a song helped the memory even more.

As to the relationship between speech and music, the children did play and did learn to play musical instruments. We have counterparts today: the quena (flute), zamponas (panpipes), wankara (drum) and pototo (conch shell horn).

Children as well as adults were entranced by the itinerant Yatriri. In Quechua language the term meant "folk healer and keeper of the legends." He told of Inca history and myth and supernatural. He traveled from ayllu to ayllu (colony to colony) and stayed at each as long as he was in demand. He was especially popular at festivals and on holidays. The Yatriri was often accompanied by musicians, a happy group of entertainers who played and danced and sang.

Yes, life was bountiful. It afforded time for leisure and play. It provided time for creativity in arts and craftsmanship. Their remarkable resourcefulness in design and crafting in gold and ceramics resulted in a demand by the Inca chieftains for more and more. Thus the more talented artisans were given full-time high-level assignments.

Chapter 13

Superb Inventors

Who developed the greatest stonework in the world?
Egyptians? Greeks? Romans? Not quite. It was the Incas,
their subjects, and their predecessors who led the world
in stonework. Their quarries were sophisticated. Their
ability to move tremendous blocks of stone from quarry
to destination was unbelievable. And their fitting of huge
multi-sided blocks into walls, with perfect joinery, is unparalleled. No other culture has come close to matching
the magnificent stonework of these people. No modern
expert has come up with a workable explanation of how
they did it, without steel tools or machinery. In their
earthquake country, their structures held. Later Spanish
structures in the same locations didn't. And this is but
one example of inventiveness.

   The Incas had need for rope to build suspension
(hanging) bridges, and for towing their quarried stone.
For the latter task they needed something strong enough
to stand the pull of a thousand men. So they learned to

twist the fibres of the Cabuya plant, something like a century plant. The resulting strands were twisted in the opposite direction, into cords—the cords into rope and the ropes into larger ropes until they had one strong enough for the job at hand. The ropes serving as cables for their suspension bridges were a foot or so thick. A series of cables became the supporting structure for the roadway capable of use by natives as well as their llamas and their loads. Thornton Wilder's *Bridge of San Luis Rey* describes such a bridge across the Apurimac River. John Roebling managed to build such a suspension bridge, twisting steel wires into cables, four hundred years later. The Incas also had fixed bridges and floating bridges —truly remarkable.

Early Asiatic and European countries exchanged ideas. The Romans, for instance, took the developments of others and improved on them. So far as we know, the Incas had no outside help. No access to libraries. No consultants. Just native ability to recognize a problem and find an answer.

The Incas deemed it necessary to establish a communication network. This required roads and way stations and messengers and, of course, bridges. The Romans, masters of road building, would have envied their achievements. But despite their resourcefulness the Incas never invented the wheel and therefore had no carts or wagons. The llama, their beast of burden, couldn't carry much cargo. Accordingly, Inca roads went as straight as possible, right up over hills and into canyons, for the animals and the messengers could run up and down slopes. They were trained for their very occupation. Nevertheless, Inca roads were ahead of their time and some are still in use.

The Inca nations, thanks to their predecessors, had remarkably advanced agriculture. In their mountainous country they built aqueducts and terraced the hillsides. The canals and ditches serving the terraces had just the right slopes—not so steep as to cause erosion, not so flat as to silt up or become saline. Whereas some civilizations had to work full-time to grow enough food, the Incas grew an excess and stored enough, as insurance against possible famine because of adverse weather. All this at high altitudes where seasons were short. They developed the sweet potato and some forty other varieties of potato, squash, beans, peanuts, fruits such as strawberries, pineapples, avocados, and mulberries. Even chocolate. Many of our modern vegetables and fruits had their genesis in Inca country. Nature was bountiful, thanks to their industry and ingenuity. They also grew and used coca, which we'll discuss in another chapter.

During their leisure time the Incas held harvest celebrations and indulged themselves in various arts and crafts, working in gold, silver, ceramics, and textiles. These attained such high importance that the artisans became specialists and were commissioned by the chieftains to devote full time to their creative work.

By trial and error, they developed the blast furnace for melting gold and other precious metals. They learned to alloy copper and tin to make bronze, "hardened copper," which was a vast improvement for cutting edges.

Not all creative work was done with the hands. They were thinkers. Although they had no written symbols, they had a decimal system used particularly in their "computer," the quipu. The quipu was an assembly of knotted strings, used to record all manner of data—census counts, tallies of harvests, animals, and even calendar events. The strings were of predetermined lengths and colors. Even the direction of twisting was controlled. Knots were tied where desired. Thus they could count in tens, hundreds, and thousands and could preserve the record. The quipu was as close to recorded language as the Incas achieved. It may have had uses not yet understood, because the Spanish, fearing that they were diabolical devices, did away with them. Those now in existence have been found in tombs.

They also had the concept of zero. It is strange that such a brilliant people had no written language. They must not have sensed the need for it.

The Incas excelled in the construction of reed boats. Reeds (totora grass) were plentiful in Lake Titicaca. The stems being hollow with partitions, they floated. It seems perfectly natural that they would be bundled and used as rafts. But the Incas went further. They developed a boat with a distinctive high prow and stern. Then, needing a floating bridge, they fixed a rope across a waterway, tied successive boats to it and assembled a roadway—a true pontoon bridge.

Individual balsa boats of giant size were suitable for ocean voyages. With a service life of some two years before the reeds became waterlogged, it was possible to go great distances, say, to the South Seas. How else did the sweet potato get transported to South Pacific islands?

The balsa boat inspired even larger craft. Searching for buoyancy of a larger dimension, the pre-Incas found that the logs of the ochroma tree were buoyant and resistant to saturation. A raft of logs would be lashed together and a small house built on the deck. They rigged mast and sails and were ready for trading along the coast.

Another device, the loom, permitted intricate weaving. There is nothing in nature that they could have copied, so again, the Incas and their forebears are credited with invention.

How about the field of medicine? Early peoples, including the Peruvians, mixed the supernatural with the human condition. The shaman practiced mysticism along with practical healing. Without their recognizing it as such, this involved psychology—belief that disease was being overcome on the part of the ailing person.

In addition, Peruvian natives were extremely resourceful in finding out which plant could alleviate what disease. To find out which were poisonous and which were beneficial must have taken a toll. But gradually the number of beneficial herbs, barks, saps, and other substances grew to be a virtual pharmacy. Quinine, belladonna, tobacco, ipecac—all had their special uses and still do. For energy, the coca plant was invaluable but, as mentioned, we'll talk about this later.

Surgery was not unknown to these people. The most hazardous and intricate operation was trepanning. Broken skulls from hand weapons used in tribal conflicts must have been frequent. In any event, early surgeons were successful in using bronze tools to cut openings in the cranium to relieve pressure, remove fragments, or cure infection. How do we know? In tombs, both bronze tools and trepanned skulls have been found. What a remarkable achievement for these "primitive" people! They were not only inventors—they cared about their fellow man.

But the most devastating chapter of health history is about the diseases that white man and Western natives gave to each other. We will discuss this later.

Chapter 14

A Love Affair

Inca Roca, sixth of the Inca Emperors, ruled with traditional power. He encouraged better agriculture and artistry with gold and silver and ceramics. Under his leadership crops were more than adequate—so bountiful that some was burned each year as a tribute to the gods. Gold mines were producing more than could be made into replicas of plants and animals and humans. Walls in royal areas were tiled with gold plaques. Walks were paved with gold. The untarnished brilliance of royal areas was dazzling even at dawn and dusk. These were happy days.

Inca Roca also adhered to the principle of population growth, to provide farmers, warriors, workers, and artisans. Thus sexual activity was encouraged. Such freedom resulted in boastful exploits and experimentation. Adolescents were expected to become intimately acquainted.

Inca Roca had an advantage—he had many wives in the royal court. They enjoyed each other to the fullest. And he started a collection of ceramic vases depicting all manner of intimate man-woman embraces. Some of these may be seen today in private museums in Lima.

Mamani, chief pottery maker, was hard at work. "Just a little faster, Yma." He was using a ceramic disc as an improvised potter's wheel and his helper was rotating it. Mamani had stumbled onto this device accidentally. Wanting a symmetrical vase, more precise than was possible with hand molding, he conceived a rotating platform that could rotate while his hands formed the vase. He resorted to what he knew best—baked clay. So he made the large disc with a hole in the middle to receive a pivot. It worked. But he didn't realize that he had made a wheel that might have revolutionized Inca transport. To this day it is commonly known that the wheel was never invented in the Inca nation.

Mamani's name meant "hawk," of little significance except that he did have an eagle eye for detail and was unerringly perceptive. He was married and had two energetic children whom he adored. They played together whenever possible—games of tag or tossing pebbles to see who could come closest to a line drawn on the ground. He had become the leading artisan in the ceramic group through merit. He knew where to find the best clay, how to prepare it for working, how to build objects with coils or pressing or molding, and how to fire in his improvised oven. So Inca Roca had commissioned him to make an endless variety of erotic vases and had provided him with a special workplace and a beautiful young helper, Yma.

Yma's twin sister had been selected as one of the Chosen Women. For some unexplained reason only one of the twins had been so recruited—perhaps to limit selections to one per family. So Yma, equally beautiful and bright, was a "left-out" girl and was assigned to the ceramic group as a worker. She enjoyed her role and soon became expert in the various steps of pottery making. In "smashing" clay to remove pebbles and various impurities, she preferred working it with her bare feet, sensitive to feeling things to be discarded. She loved squishing the mud between her toes. She gathered firewood and knew how to develop just the right temperature in the kiln. She was ever so responsive to helping the artisans, especially Mamani whom she secretly adored.

Mamani was far from being oblivious to Yma's charms, though he gave no thought to her attractiveness other than to realize how fortunate he was to have such a beautiful assistant. He appreciated the quickness of her learning each task. Perhaps some day she too might become a master artisan.

Selecting just the right clay was no easy task. Mamani taught his helper to dig alongside the stream where it flattened out into a sort of meadow. There was a suitable clay that, when nearly dried and then puddled and worked to the right consistency, could be fired without fracturing, though sometimes it had too much sand and crumbled. Yma was an avid learner.

She also paid close attention to Mamani's sculpturing of his vases and he liked her coming close to study his creations. She even became so bold as to make an occasional suggestion—how he might make an erotic scene even more adventurous. Such was no surprise, for she, like her contemporaries, knew much. But when her garment brushed innocently against Mamani's shoulder it aroused him. The fragrance of the flower in her hair stimulated desire. Mamani was falling in love. Day by day he tried to put amorous thoughts out of his mind. And day by day the magnetism grew stronger. Yma sensed his yearning but didn't realize its insistence.

Over a period of weeks and months Mamani produced many vases to the delight of his emperor. Each was unique, depicting highly imaginative man-woman intimacies. The fact that some were physically impossible was no deterrent—it merely added incentive to the beholder. And over those same weeks and months Mamani realized that he had fallen in love. Here was a new dimension in his life, unlike anything he had ever experienced. Thoughts of Yma became an obsession.

Love for Yma did inspire more creativity. But his erotic themes, if anything, intensified his personal arousal. He engraved scenes into nearly dry vases, then filled the grooves with clay of a different color. When fired, they were spectacular. He sculpted magnificent figures and glued them with liquid clay onto vases fresh from the potter's wheel. Yma became fascinated. Mamani became more and more impassioned.

One day he called her over and said, "Yma, this is my masterpiece. See this coupling that only true lovers might enjoy? See how these two almost become one? Don't tell anyone, but this is you and me. For months I have wanted to tell you that you mean more to me than life itself. I can't remain silent any longer else I would destroy myself. And I have an idea. I think there is some special clay a little farther downstream than we have been going, on the edge of the forest. Let's go down there tomorrow, and while we're there, let's . . ."

"Oh, Mamani!" Yma was startled, though not surprised. She too had thought how nice it would be if they could enjoy each other. But she was disciplined by knowing the severity of the sentence on being detected. "How beautiful. Could I have it for my very own? You are wonderful, but shouldn't we wait? Perhaps some day the feeling will pass."

"Yma, I'm willing to take the risk. And anyway, who will know if we don't tell? Tomorrow, then?" And he carefully placed the masterpiece on the shelf to dry for a few days before firing.

That night as Mamani and Yma, in their separate beds, dreamt of love, there came a rumbling, then a roar, then the earth trembled. The volcano had blown its top, causing an earthquake and triggering an avalanche so destructive that it erased an entire neighboring village. Come daylight Mamani hastened to the workshop. It was a shambles. There stood Yma, clutching the shattered masterpiece. "Oh, what a tragedy. Our treasure is broken."

"Yma, the gods have given us a message not to go downstream seeking clay. But I want the gods to know that they have not shattered my love for you."

Chapter 15

Expedition South

Vasco Balboa and Francisco Pizarro, having reached the Pacific, had talked at length about sailing downcoast in quest of gold. Balboa, being more perceptive, had a better understanding from the Panamanian natives as to what to expect. Gold? Vast quantities. They knew this from those who had seen it. Good sailing? Yes, between storms. Coastwise balsa vessels had traded along the coast for centuries. Balboa's having visited the Pearl Islands didn't help much, for they were just over the horizon, still in the huge Gulf of Panama. Even the Gulf of San Miguel he had visited was only about seventy-five miles downcoast. He also knew that the natives could be unfriendly but that he had found ways to gain their support. Pizarro hadn't learned the niceties of diplomacy. Force and threats were his means of getting his way.

The planners had ample reason for not attempting an expedition by land. Previous parties had tried and had had to give up. Impenetrable jungle was the principal impediment. And swamps adjacent to rivers were formidable.

Panamanian Governor Pedrarias Davila, himself an intrepid explorer, encouraged an expedition to the south. This was the opportunity Pizarro wanted. His competitor, Balboa, had been eliminated.

So Pizarro recruited two partners: Diego de Almagro and Padre Hernando do Luque, Bishop of Panama. Pizarro was to command. Almagro was the organizer. Luque was to raise the necessary funds. The three would share equally in any spoils, after setting aside the Crown's share. The Governor issued them a permit to "explore and conquer." As soon as Father Luque raised enough money, Almagro purchased one of the brigantines built by Balboa. Pizarro departed in November, 1524, with eighty soldiers, four horses, a couple of canoes, and supplies including trinkets to appease the natives. Almagro stayed behind to recruit more soldiers. So, thirty-two years after the Great Discovery, the search south for gold was under way—they thought.

Pizarro was no sailor and apparently hadn't inspected his ship to find that its planking had been riddled by borers. First day out the ship became waterlogged. They made it to the Pearl Islands where it sank. Why hadn't they gone back to Panama? There they were, marooned and scowled at by a colony of hostile cannibals in a forest of huge trees. They decided to build a new ship, salvaging what they could from the sunken brigantine and hewing new planking from felled trees. After a couple of years they were well along with construction when it was realized that they needed pitch to seal seams and iron to double-nail the planking. The closest supply was Acla on the Caribbean side where the original ship had been prefabricated. Incomplete but navigable, they limped to Panama—after three years of hunger, mosquitoes, and cannibal threats. What a stupid waste of three years!

Governor Davila had become Governor of Nicaragua and had been succeeded by Governor Don Pedro de los Rios. The new Governor opposed another expedition, so Pizarro and his associates decided to seek a commission

from Emperor Charles V. (Queen Isabella had died.) This involved a return to Spain. Pizarro left Nombre de Dios in 1528, taking with him some "Indians" one of whom, Felipillo, had become a reasonably good interpreter. He also took gold, silver, pearls and, to the amazement of his countrymen, several llamas. The treasure whetted appetites for more. Pizarro was fifty-seven, an old man for such ambitions. But despite all odds he never wavered from his obsession—gold.

The following year he obtained his license after professing loyalty to the Crown and urging the spread of

Catholicism. He also negotiated concessions for himself to the exclusion of his partners. Now he was ready to return to the Indies. Did he take priests to spread the gospel? Instead, he took his no-good brothers and a half-brother.

On his return the governor was distressed that he had been overruled. Almagro and Luque were angry that their partner had taken care of himself while double-crossing them. The obstreperous Pizarro brothers intensified the friction.

By 1532 the New World had been known for forty years. It took this long to launch the *real* conquest of the Incas. Hardly a soul was still around who had witnessed all the many trials and errors and the realization that the West Indies wasn't Japan. Columbus was gone, as was Queen Isabella. Balboa was all but forgotten. Some natives had been converted to Christianity, but precious few. A cathedral had been built in Panama City, however.

Francisco Pizarro was sixty-one but still full of bravado and determination. He now had his brothers, whom he felt he could trust. He relied on interpreter Felipillo, not realizing that translations were beginning to be embellished with treachery. He had his new titles of Governor and Captain General and a contract that assured wealth and prominence once he had attained his objective. He had more experience in the New World than anyone else. This time he was not to be denied success.

So, on September 24, 1532, Pizarro and his partner Almagro, with about 180 men, 67 of whom were mounted, set sail. No one wished him bon voyage. The party had two small cannons and three harquebusses. The latter were heavy flintlock guns. For firing, the barrel had to be supported on a "hook." For more than a month they followed the coastline south, stopping occasionally to trade with natives and to learn what they could about what lay ahead.

About a thousand miles south of Panama they were blown ashore. A detachment of soldiers took horses and followed a trail. They came to a colony of natives who, with their chief, had prepared a welcome and had assembled a treasury of gold, silver, and emeralds, expecting to trade. But the natives hadn't expected to see the unbelievable—horses, armor, and white complexions. This must be an act of the supernatural and a return of the legendary white men with beards. They panicked and fled, abandoning the chief and his treasure.

The ships anchored in a sheltered cove near Tumbes. It is now named Puerto Pizarro. They found Tumbes sacked and went south, where they established a base and named it Miguel de Tangarrara, a name so poetic that it should be sung. From there a guide would take them for an audience with Inca Atahuallpa. It was a tortuous trek from sea level to a valley amidst high mountains. The Inca road, having been built for pedestrians and llamas, was in places too steep for horses. Soldiers, encumbered with armor and armament also had problems. But the spirit of adventure and anticipation of what was to come urged them on. They would not be disappointed.

Chapter 16

The Conquest

Pizarro was unaware that an Inca civil war had just been concluded. For the first time in all Inca history the empire had been divided in two. Huascar and Atahualpa, sons of the deceased emperor, ruled and were soon in contention. A war erupted. Atahualpa won. With his army he was returning south to Cuzco and decided to make a rest stop at the glorious hot springs of Cajamarca. Then he would march the last 750 miles to proclaim himself Emperor of the entire Inca domain. The last leg of the triumphal trip would take about two months, high in the Andes, across deep canyons and via rope suspension bridges over raging torrents.

Atahualpa lived in the style of his ancestors, with a huge court of advisers, messengers, servants, guards, and a sizable harem of Chosen Women and their handmaidens. He was surrounded by his army. He was transported in a canopied litter borne by stalwart men who were relayed at intervals. His word was law. He was the law!

The Spaniards, as we have just related, completed the harrowing trip and arrived at Cajamarca without loss of man or beast. The Inca army was encamped on the hillside. By quick estimate they outnumbered the Spaniards about two hundred to one. The conquistadores dared not show fear, nor could they escape if they tried—all routes had been cut off. While they waited in the plaza, Atahualpa arrived, being borne on a gold litter and surrounded by hundreds of supporters. Messengers had told the emperor that he was to meet the emissary of the king of a country he had never heard of.

The Spaniards had decided to find a way to capture Atahualpa. Dominican friar Valverde approached him with cross and prayer book extended. Through interpreter Felipillo he lectured the emperor on Christianity and the necessity of his adopting the faith and acknowledging the supreme being. Atahualpa would have none of it. He already had a supreme being. Valverde was repulsed.

The Spanish, knowing of the awe with which horses were viewed, gave a brilliant display of horsemanship. Then suddenly they blasted with bugles, fired guns, shouted a war cry "Santiago," drew swords and took Atahualpa into custody before startled guards and litter carriers could react.

While he was held captive and knowing that the Spanish were seeking gold and silver, Atahualpa offered a deal. For his release he would give them a roomful of gold and twice as much silver, all expertly crafted. It would come to Cajamarca from Cuzco. Pizarro accepted. Transport required five months. By mid-1533 more than twenty-four *tons* of treasures had been delivered. The Spaniards were ecstatic. The entire lot except for a few exceptional pieces for the king was melted into ingots. This required an additional two months. Each soldier was given forty-five pounds of gold and ninety of silver—more than he could carry. Some lightened their loads by gambling them away, thus doubling the loads of the winners. The king's portion would go over that tortuous route to Tumbes, by ship to Panama, across the isthmus, and then across the Atlantic to Spain.

The Spaniards had no appreciation of the rarity and value of those marvelous artifacts. Vases and jewelry and replicas of birds and animals and flowers were lost to the world. It is even reported that the Spanish king, after receiving his gifts, had them melted down and minted. The collection would have filled many museums, with value beyond comprehension. Sole tribute was the construction of Iglesia de San Francisco (Church of St. Francis) in Cajamarca, the first Christian edifice in Peru.

Pizarro and Almagro, in one of their rare agreements, decided that Atahualpa was not to be trusted and that he should be eliminated. They falsely accused him of conspiring to exterminate the Spaniards. They condemned him to death—and kept the loot that he had provided for his freedom. At that same time, a comet crossed the heavens. According to Inca superstition this portended disaster. Atahualpa sensed the seriousness of his plight. He was given the option of death by burning or, if he became a Christian, by garroting. He chose the latter, adopted the name Francisco, was baptized, then garroted. One more soul for Christianity.

Without their omnipotent dictator the Inca army and colony were shocked into speechlessness and inaction. Pizarro would be the new emperor. Later he would be chastised for taking the life of a head of state. Pizarro must have gloated over how his bravado had conquered the Incas but never realized how lucky he had been.

Now he could go to Cuzco and take over the capital. With good guides his contingent, which was by now adapted to exertion at high altitudes, might get there in as little as five weeks. This would require foraging, sending cavalrymen ahead to select campsites and scout for possible ambush. Hopefully, suspension bridges, such as the one over the Apurimac, would be passable. One can't help but respect Pizarro's resolve. At his age of sixty-three, very few if any conquistadores would even be alive.

Taking over Cuzco was easy. Word had already passed that he, the governor, was now the successor to the Supreme Inca. And gold, vast quantities of it, remained intact, available for the taking.

Now was the time for Governor Pizarro to return to Spain to report to the king and receive deserved plaudits. He left his brother Gonzalo in charge and named Prince Manco as puppet Inca.

Meanwhile, Almagro had taken a small force and interpreter Felipillo to explore and claim lands southward, following Inca roads. He went as far as the present Santiago, Chile.

On his return from Spain, Pizarro founded Lima, Peru, on January 18, 1535. The Spanish population in Peru was increasing, but peace was yet to come. Manco Inca, feeling that he had been deceived (perhaps with the advice of Felipillo who was privy to Spanish confidentialities), attempted a military takeover. It was unsuccessful.

Almagro and Pizarro still contended. In a fracas Almagro was captured and put to death. Almagro's son swore vengeance and in due course helped assassinate Francisco Pizarro on January 26, 1541.

Foment continued among Spanish factions—stabbings, double-crossings, imprisonments, intrigue. Even the clergy got involved. Then Francisco de Toledo was named Viceroy and served in that office for thirteen years. He pacified the Incas and maintained a strong rule over the Spaniards. He opened mines and transferred great wealth to Spain. He enhanced the position of the Church. His pattern continued for 250 years, up to the time of the War of Independence.

Chapter 17
The Dilemma of a Unified Church and State

Speaking of doing things the hard way, a country dedicated to Christianizing the infidels of a previously unknown territory was at the same time dedicated to con-
quering, establishing rule, and seizing wealth in that
same territory. The first principle was in the direction of
peace; the second would lead to war. Spain wanted both.

The Pope had ordered Spain to save the souls of the
heathens and the Spanish monarchs wanted that responsibility. Isabella and Ferdinand were pledged to Catholicize their own country, and that included all of its do-
mains. They would send friars to indoctrinate and baptize
those innocent people. In so doing they would earn the
everlasting blessing of God. But they misjudged their
own people. They should have known better. The Spanish

populace at that time was not geared for high principles and many of those who hastened to America were the least trustworthy. Some of the clergy who went and reveled in their new freedom joined the life of their contemporaries. They should have turned in their robes. Those of the clergy who adhered to high principles had difficulty in making any headway.

The queen and king were enticed by the prospect of gold, which would relieve their sagging economy. Encouraged by their court to colonize the new territory, they sent parties but made very sad choices. Busy as they were, they saw no alternative to governing directly—that is, retaining the right to make decisions on highly important matters. Calling the shots halfway around the world with a round-trip time lapse of at least a year was a tremendous handicap. Circumstances would have changed before a problem could be answered. But even worse, Their Highnesses could not witness the situation personally. Had they, their reaction to the virtual defection of their countrymen would have been instantaneous. And had they been seen by their New World subjects, their very presence would have reaffirmed loyalties to the crown and a commitment to peace and prosperity.

Maltreatment of the natives was widespread. One friar who took exception to the practice was unique. On a Sunday he preached against such conduct. The congregation protested and demanded an apology. The friar's response was to repeat the sermon on the following Sunday. A fiery protest was sent to the Council of the Indies. The dispatch must have warped the truth, for by return mail (weeks later) the governor was ordered to reason with the friar. He was warned that no more friars would be sent to the New World if such preaching were to continue. The master/servant relationship was countenanced. No mention of maltreatment.

The Spaniards assumed the right to control the lives of the natives, justified by the counterbalancing responsibility of the natives to respond to conversion. So serious were the Spaniards about this principle that they developed it into a legal authenticity. Legal with the Spaniards, that is. The natives weren't consulted. It became known as the encomienda. Learning of this, Queen Isabella objected. To her, the natives belonged to the Crown, not to the settlers. The natives were to receive fair pay for their work and were to be treated as free persons, not as slaves. The settlers reacted by demanding tribute from the natives—a return of the wages for the Christianizing they received! Then the ecclesiastics became legalistic and won a point: the natives were to serve for a limited period of time, not for life, thus solving the problem of slavery. That didn't sell either. So, for the first twenty years or so of Spanish rule, the exploitation of natives was almost unchecked.

The cardinal appointed Bartolome de las Casas as "Protector of the Indians" and sent him back to America. He was a Dominican friar who had become a highly vocal champion of the natives and accused his countrymen of horrible cruelty. Arriving in Hispaniola, he was confronted with continued hostility of the settlers and an official inquiry by royal officials. Twelve of the oldest inhabitants were each asked seven questions. "Should the natives be given complete liberty? Would they be able to support themselves? Would they have use for any wages they might receive?"—and the like. You can guess the answers. Again the friars failed to correct their countrymen.

Other attempts were made, such as by Judge Rodrigo de Figueroa in 1518. By this time the population of natives had dwindled because of white man's diseases. Although he did manage to free some natives, his efforts were mostly futile.

There was a unique reversal of affairs in Santiago. The natives had been so maltreated that they rebelled and escaped to remote places. The friars charged with Christianizing them could therefore make no headway. In frustration they called on the settlers for help to punish the natives. The Spaniards said "nothing doing," citing the royal order forbidding them to interfere with the "Indians" or to enter their territory.

Another strange edict was issued in Chile. Pizarro's conquistadores had been so brutal with the natives that a Dominican friar beseeched that "war against the Araucanian Indians not be made cruelly or barbarously but with humanity and justice"! Nevertheless, the Jesuits, Franciscans, and Dominicans agreed, for once, that the enslavement of the natives was warranted.

By the end of the sixteenth century the inevitable question arose as to whether Spain was entitled to legal possession of its overseas territories. Throughout history, the conqueror has always claimed the land of the conquered—but this was not the immediate issue. Rather, the question was whether Spain had a valid mandate to conquer.

THE CROWN: Spain had complied with the Papal Bull. The Pope had given the New World for the conversion of the natives. Spain had carefully and legally provided for conversions and good treatment.

ARCOS, A DOMINICAN OF SEVILLE: The Christian Princes had no more authority over the infidels with papal authorization than without it.

JIMINEZ QUESADA: After all, the ground the Spanish tread on belongs to the natives. They allow us a favor to be here and owe us nothing.

DOMINICAN VITORIA: The Emperor was not the lord of the whole world and neither was the Pope. But Spaniards have the right to preach and declare the gospel in barbarian lands.

VICEROY TOLEDO: The Inca rule was never recognized voluntarily by the natives, but was obeyed through fear. Thus, Spanish rule was necessary and just.

LAS CASAS: The Pope had no authority to force infidels to accept Christianity and therefore could not bestow such power on the Spanish kings. Nor did the Pope have authority to punish the sins of non-Christians.

A FRANCISCAN: Dear Lord enlighten us so that we might cease to live in sin and begin to live for righteousness.

ANOTHER FRANCISCAN: My countrymen want to love the natives in heaven—but not before.

The hubbub went on and on and on. But it brought out clearly that no nation ever took Christianity as seriously as did Spain. The framers of the U.S. Constitution and the Bill of Rights were guided by Spanish experience: Amendment 1—"Congress shall make no law respecting an establishment of religion, or prohibiting the free exercise thereof. . . ." Thus church and state are, and should be, separate.

Chapter 18
Tragic Reciprocity

Smallpox, measles, and mumps have been normal childhood diseases for centuries. Until recently, every youngster was expected to contract them, be sick for a short while, recover, and stay recovered. The illness was usually not very severe and an immunity developed to prevent recurrence. Not so with the natives of the Western Hemisphere. They had never had these diseases and their immune systems were not prepared for such invasion. Unwittingly, the Spaniards were carriers. Initial cases developed into epidemics. Cases were so serious that deaths were widespread. Brilliant as they were in finding remedies, white man's diseases arrived too suddenly to a people that had no safeguard and no concept of what they were. What with their mysticism, they might even have thought it the vengeance of an unseen enemy.

No statistical records were kept until centuries later for the Tierra del Fuegans (Yahgans) who suffered from the visits of the Magellan and Charles Darwin parties. Darwin's time: 3,000 souls and by 1884 fewer than 1,000; soon thereafter, 400; by 1908, 170; by 1943, 43. In all innocence, neither the carriers nor the victims knew what was going on. The toll was much more severe than losses due to conquest.

Equally innocent, Columbus took several "Indians" back to Spain as exhibits. He didn't know that they might have been contaminated with a venereal disease and might spread it. More likely, Columbus's crew, who found native women ever so hospitable, contracted the disease and carried it back to Spain in 1493. It spread throughout the country, then to Italy and France, all of Europe, and all of the "civilized" world.

Syphilis emanates from sexual activity. It starts with a germ that requires warmth, moisture, and the absence of air for survival—ideal for the human genitals. It is transmitted only from a diseased person to a well person, primarily during sexual intercourse. After several weeks of incubation a sore appears, which soon becomes a chancre that expands to one or two inches in diameter. Infection spreads throughout the body, affecting the mucous membranes, causing headaches and achy joints and loss of energy. Without medical attention, it may cause death.

There is no evidence that the Incas had found a cure for syphilis. Certainly the Europeans hadn't. Today penicillin, properly administered, is effective.

Several factors delayed the control of the disease—first, a feeling of disgrace and desire for secrecy on the part of the victim. Many an innocent person was thus contaminated. There was reluctance to divulge the disease even to a doctor. Second, a cessation of visible evidences several weeks after the initial sores, which deluded victims into feeling that the disease had passed. And, finally, a lack of realization that the disease subtly and silently deteriorated the body to a point where it was impossible to cure.

We have mentioned malaria in another chapter. It is another example of transfer of disease to newcomers who weren't prepared for it and misinterpreted its cause.

All this: tragic reciprocity.

Chapter 19
Coca—Cocaine

Long before the dawn of civilization in the Eastern Hemisphere the natives of the Western Hemisphere, particularly in what became Peru, were picking up alluvial gold because it was attractive, and picking leaves of the coca plant to chew because it seemed good. Both were important to their way of life, some seven thousand years ago. A worker with a quid of coca leaves in his cheek looked like he had a toothache. But he had no pain, only pleasure. As a pain deadener and hunger suppressor, it made their vigorous lives tolerable at high altitudes. It actually reduced fatigue. And the practice of swallowing saliva infused with coca has continued there ever since.

During the ensuing centuries the natives learned that powdered chalk of pulverized seashells would enhance the effect. Gourds with swizzle sticks became portable containers. In use, the stick was moistened with spit, dipped into the lime and probed into the quid. Every man carried a gourd or ceramic bottle (poporo). And when ceremonies developed to usher a youth into the responsibilities of manhood, the subject's ears were pierced, some proofs of manhood were ritualized, and a poporo was awarded. Holes in the earlobes were gradually enlarged with bigger and bigger plugs, as was his appetite for coca. He always carried his poporo. The ruling Inca had a gold one although coca was considered more valuable than gold, silver, or precious stones.

When the Spanish arrived they noticed the value placed on coca and were quick to introduce it back home. Sure enough, they soon had a market. This required larger and larger coca plantations—easy to arrange, what with free labor. Lucrative trade grew. Even the Church got into the act. As Piedro Cieza de Leon wrote, "The greater portion of the income of the bishop, canons, and other clergy was from coca."

When my Carmen and I arrived in Cuzco one midday and checked in at our hotel intending to drop our luggage and go exploring on a beautiful sunny day, the manager advised us to have some tea and lie down for a couple of hours to adjust to the altitude (some twelve thousand feet). We said, "We feel fine—and what's tea got to do with it?" He said, "This is coca tea, which helps you accommodate to our two-mile height. Everyone does it." We refused politely, had a quick lunch and took our walk through that enchanting city. No ill effects. But others followed the advice and felt the better for it.

We knew something about narcotics and wanted to know more—short of indulging. It started with a question: "How come Peruvians use coca as a beneficial sedative, while others using cocaine from the same plant ruin their lives?" Modern chemists provide the answer. The difference is like day and night. The quid routine, extracting only a tiny amount of cocaine is a hunger and pain deadener and is even used as an anesthetic. But purified cocaine, inhaled or injected, can be lethal. One would think that a mixture of carbon, hydrogen, nitrogen and oxygen shouldn't be bad. Yet cocaine $C_{17} H_{21} NO_4$

is one of the world's enemies. Coca leaves contain four types of alkaloids, two of which are sources of cocaine.

The conversion from coca leaves to cocaine is not complicated. Dump green leaves into a plastic-lined pit containing water and sulfuric acid. After stirring it once in a while for three or four days, take off the liquid in plastic buckets and discard the smelly mash. Add to the buckets your own favorite recipe of (believe it or not) lime water, gasoline, sulfuric acid, potassium permanganate and ammonia. If it hasn't blown up or eaten a hole in the plastic, add more ammonia and filter out the crystals that have just formed. When dry, the product is cocaine base, ready for export.

Early "chemistry" was preceded by the quick uptake of the patent medicine and soft drink people. Customers would buy any bottle that purported to cure the vapors or shakes. Taking it, they felt better, too. Why not? Those bottles contained boosters like Lydia Pinkham's Vegetable Compound that had an unadvertised percentage of alcohol. Some users were teetotalers, members of the WCTU. As for narcotics, the original Coca-Cola contained cocaine, as did others joining in the rush for users, like Koca-Kola, Kos-Kola, Coke Extract, Kola Ale, Celery Cola, Rococola, Wiseola, Dr. Doris Kola, and perhaps others. Legislation phased them out, except for Coca-Cola which eliminated the cocaine but retained the flavor.

Today, cocaine is used legally by the medical profession—for instance, in nasal surgery where it is both a local anesthetic and a blood vessel constrictor.

But cocaine hydrochloride and its several derivatives, like freebase and crack, sold illegally, are devastating the United States and other countries. Smoked, snorted, or injected, it hits the brain in seconds and wears off in minutes, only to create a need for more. Users become addicts. It ruins lives. It attracts criminals and creates more criminals. Billions of dollars change hands, attracting gangs and the Mafia. Elimination of both supply and demand is a high priority national issue. As this is written one can only hope that international control can come fast—and that the Peruvians and their neighbors can find an alternate for their profitable crops, saving some coca leaves for their historical usage.

Chapter 20
From Then On

From the time of the conquest, South America evolved to its present world prominence, but not easily. The Spanish maintained their dominance for nearly three hundred years and even muscled into Portuguese territory. During the most recent two hundred years there were arguments, disputes, dissentions, and armed conflicts too numerous to mention. If recalled, they would make for sometimes exciting but mostly boring reading. And there were some brilliant highlights.

Historic incidents, though sometimes related to geology or nature, primarily involve leaders. Some of them in South America were exceedingly colorful and significant.

Take Sir Henry John Morgan. Recall that the British were quick to become involved in the Caribbean soon after there was a New World. They were traders who also needed a few footholds. And since their shipping had to contend with piracy, they fought fire with fire. Sir Henry was a buccaneer. He came into his trade forthrightly. Born in Wales, he was kidnapped at an early age and sold in Barbados. There he became a seafarer and learned all the tricks of the trade. In his twenties he commanded his own ship. At age thirty he was an admiral.

Morgan heard that the Spanish were readying to attack Jamaica. To learn about their plans he captured Puerto Principe, then went on to Porto Bello, Panama, where he sacked the city and tortured the inhabitants. His entry into the fortress was most resourceful: his crew planted scaling ladders under the cover of captured priests and nuns!

By 1671 Morgan was thirty-six and a seasoned buccaneer, respected and feared by all who knew of him. To keep the trade route open across the Isthmus of Panama he assumed the task of ousting the Spanish from Panama City. This, obviously, was no seaborne maneuver. Morgan and his force became land soldiers, crossed the isthmus and engaged in pitched battle with the Spanish who, of course, knew he was coming. The Spanish cavalry charged and very adroitly were forced into a swamp where horses couldn't do much more than wallow. Then, the Spanish released a herd of cattle to break the English ranks. As if by magic the herd was diverted and stampeded right into the Spanish. Even the caballeros who had survived the running of the bulls in Pamplona couldn't withstand this. Morgan sacked Panama City and the trade route was secured. Then, having had enough of a life-endangering career, Morgan became a landlubber in Jamaica where he was named Lieutenant Governor.

Even earlier, Spanish adventurers and colonists flooded to the New World, representatives of the church included. By 1560 there were some 350 priests in Peru. But, instead of spreading Catholicism they chose the elitist life as in Spain. Conversions were few and these were mostly due to the efforts of the Spanish women who indoctrinated their servants. The natives, with their traditional rituals suppressed, were now devoid of religion and were attracted to the new one.

Then came the discovery of tremendously rich silver deposits in Potosi, in what is now Bolivia. It was so productive that it revolutionized the power and price structure of Europe and eventually financed the Industrial Revolution. But at what a price! Natives, as virtual slaves, were conscripted miners. Imagine the torturous life: forty-five hundred workers descending rawhide ladders down a 750-foot vertical shaft into hot, humid, foul darkness to a series of tunnels. There they mined ore from the tunnel face. At the end of the shift each miner carried a hundred pounds or so of ore back up the ladder. The chewing of coca leaves helped, but not enough. Sickness and deaths were common. As the local population was depleted, workers were imported from Peru and Argentina, some seven thousand persons per year just to keep up with the attrition.

Some worked in the ore processing area, topside. Even this was hazardous, for the Spanish were using mercury to absorb the silver from the crushed ore. The quicksilver was then heated and vaporized, leaving metallic silver. Result: mercury poisoning. But the mining went on. One haul in 1630 was fifty thousand *tons* of silver!

Let's take a glance at what was happening on the Atlantic side. Recall that one of Columbus's companions discovered South America: Vicente Pinzon, in 1500. This encouraged others. Amerigo Vespucci made two voyages, did some mapping, and lent his name. Then came Magellan, going into every harbor and up every navigable river, searching for a sea route to the South Sea. He found it close to the southern tip, seventy-five hundred sea miles from Panama. It was so calm, he renamed it the Pacific. The Strait of Magellan became the only route west for sailing vessels, except for rounding Cape Horn and contending with the perilous Drake Strait. How much simpler life could have been if there had been a canal through the Isthmus of Panama.

Many Europeans were attracted to the New World—Portuguese farmers grew and harvested sugar and spices. Miners found amethysts and diamonds. A thriving economy was established, and when Napoleon took over Portugal, its royal family fled to Brazil, adding prestige. The influx into Brazil was not only from Portugal but Italy, Spain, Germany, Netherlands, Russia, Austria and, believe it or not, Japan. The French tried to muscle in militarily, but were repulsed. The Dutch West India Company prospered but was finally ousted, retaining Surinam on the north coast, one of the Guianas. When warfare and pestilence depleted the working population, able bodies were needed. The obvious answer at that time was to import slaves from Africa. The English, who were veterans with this sort of commerce, were given exclusive right to provide the bodies.

As the economy grew, important industry arrived—coffee, then cattle raising. The Argentinian gaucho, part Spanish and part native, became legendary, envied for his glamorous life in the pampas.

Gradually countries were defined by often contested boundaries. Then came the quest for independence. This brings us to the story of two outstanding leaders.

José de San Martin was born in a remote Argentinian village in 1778. Both parents were Spanish. His father was governor of the mission town but was soon transferred to Buenos Aires and then to Spain. So young José grew up and was educated in Spain, including service as a military cadet. By the time he was sixteen he had not only seen combat in North Africa against the Barbary Pirates, but became a commissioned officer. During the next twenty years he saw plenty of action both on land and sea and helped defend Spain against Napoleon's forces. Several of his officer buddies became obsessed with the cause of independence and José developed a conviction that his native Argentina should be freed.

In his early thirties José resigned his commission, left Spain, and went to England and from there to his native Argentina. His dedication was phenomenal in that his parents were Spanish, his active life had been in Spain, his career had been in the very army that had to be overthrown if Argentina and its neighbors were to become independent. He had only known Argentina up to about age five. Yet he was dedicated to the liberation of Argentina from Spain. The cause for independence was that strong.

On arrival in Buenos Aires he was given permission to form a new military unit and was awarded his previous grade of lieutenant colonel. Through friends of friends he recruited an elite corps of cavalrymen, the Mounted Grenadiers. He stimulated a patriotic movement, then was placed in command of the Army of the North. He established a training center, and again his cavalrymen achieved perfection.

In studying how to defeat the Spanish headquartered in Lima, he developed a most remarkable, seemingly impossible plan: Go over the Andes into Chile, knock out the Spanish in Santiago, go by boat to Peru, then by land to fight the Spanish. Previous attempts by others, traveling traditional routes, had failed. So he established a staging area to perfect his plan.

Moving out, his army divided, one unit on each side of 22,834-foot Mount Aconcagua, the highest peak in

South America. After skirmishes, they won Chile's independence. Then, going by ship to southern Peru, he reassembled his army and ousted the Spanish from Lima. Independence Day was July 28, 1821. San Martín was declared Protector of Peru, an office he was loath to accept.

Meanwhile Simón Bolívar had been slowly making progress in the North. Bolívar was politically oriented, using military force only out of necessity, whereas San Martín was a militarist who entered the political scene only reluctantly. The two had corresponded and, in fact, met in Guayaquil, Ecuador, a year after the liberation of Peru.

We all know that Bolívar is the historic liberator of much of South America. His achievements are universally honored. His dedication as a young man had been intensified when he visited the United States in his midtwenties. A year later he was back in Venezuela offering his services to the revolutionists.

Intent on extending Christianity and saving souls, Franciscan and Dominican monks had concentrated near the Venezuelan coast in the early 1500s. They had found the natives friendly and receptive. They discouraged the taking of slaves. In 150 years they had founded thirty-eight towns, supplanting tribal settlements. Each village, of course, had a church. In this atmosphere the cause of independence must have been well advanced, for after a few months of effort, Bolívar's country declared its independence—July 5, 1811, a year after Argentina's. But the Spanish were persistent and Bolívar was confronted with a series of upsets.

The prospect of winning permanent peace was so discouraging to the new leader that he, at one stage, resigned his commission. He was urged to continue the war and was made commander-in-chief. Then he had the good fortune to win some battles in this vast, forbidding region. He joined forces with the leader of New Granada to the west. This resulted into the merging of Venezuela and New Granada into a new country named Colombia. It even included Panama. Ecuador was added soon after. Bolívar became president and celebrated the adoption of a new constitution late in 1821, a month after Peru became free. But there were still Spanish unwilling to pack up and go home.

Bolívar and San Martín sent General Sucre on a mission to Ecuador. Quito fell to him. Bolívar went on to Lima and became president of Peru, probably on San Martín's urging. In visiting Upper Peru he saw the need for a separate state. It was named Bolivia in his honor. The Spanish were no more. Ill and exhausted, Bolívar died in 1830, aged forty-seven.

But before the two heroes retired from their historic roles they were honored at a banquet. Bolívar, confident, egotistical, politically adroit, reveled in the limelight; San Martín, militarily brilliant, politically shy, avoiding notoriety. Came the time for toasts. Bolívar: "To the two greatest men in South America—General San Martín and myself." San Martín: "To the early end of the war; to the organization of the various republics of the continent; and to the health of the liberator of Colombia."

Another figure, not often credited with leadership in the South American cause: James Monroe, fifth president of the United States. His heritage and timing were just right. He was born in 1758. At age eighteen he was a lieutenant in a Virginia regiment and fought intensively in the Revolutionary War. He engaged in volunteer efforts in behalf of his state. Then he studied law under

99

Thomas Jefferson who was then governor of Virginia and the two became close friends. Monroe served in the Virginia legislature and the Congress of the Confederation and the State convention to ratify the Federal Constitution. He became a U.S. Senator, Minister to France, Governor of Virginia. He had an active role in negotiations leading to the Louisiana Purchase and became Secretary of State. In 1816 he was elected president by a wide margin.

Despite his remarkable achievements, Monroe was not a colorful public figure. He was not a good speaker. He lacked tact and was often indiscreet. Yet people supported him and, as Teddy Roosevelt said years later; "He had greatness thrust upon him." These were turbulent times and Monroe, taking a stand on every issue, was always in contention: slavery, Indians, the Missouri Compromise, railroad problems. But his Monroe Doctrine (December 2, 1823) was different. It was received with widespread popularity.

Monroe knew that Great Britain, France, Netherlands, Sweden, and Denmark had colonies in the Western Hemisphere. Russia had Alaska. They and others were making moves for further inroads into promising lands. Yet the move for independence and self-determination was strong and growing. It seemed time to formulate and declare a position. The British, knowing of this and wanting to secure their trading advantages, proposed a joint declaration. Monroe decided to go it alone.

The Monroe Doctrine clearly opposed European powers establishing settlements or colonies in any part of the Americas or exerting undue influence. Excepted were Canada, Cuba, Puerto Rico, English and French Islands, and the three South American "plantations" (the Guianas). The Doctrine was immediately effective but soon developed an unexpected side effect—the Latin Americans expected military protection. The Doctrine withstood a test when Germany took an interest in Venezuela. It supported Teddy Roosevelt with his "Big Stick" policy. It held during the Spanish-American War when Cuba became virtually a protectorate of the United States and we acquired the Philippines. By 1830 the last of the South American nations declared independence, three hundred years after the conquistadores set foot on American soil. The Monroe Doctrine was a powerful document in behalf of the Americans until it was gradually succeeded by the Organization of American States.

We are well aware that the plight of the native was not a happy one. Nor was the life of the slave anything but pure hell. But there were those who made headway for those seeking a better life. They were persons of unprecedented courage and true devotion to the principles of Christendom. Among them were ladies who cared for the poor, the maimed, and the sick, and who grew very close to the church. Some lived such exemplary lives as to warrant sainthood. We think of two: Isabel de Flores y Olivia (St. Rose of Lima) and Mariana Paredes y Flores (St. Lily of Quito).

Isabel was born in Lima when it was a tiny settlement founded by Francisco Pizarro, who had been deposed and assassinated by those whom he had offended. Francisco's brother, Gonzalo, had proclaimed himself governor. Lima then settled down to a more or less peaceful existence. Lima "downtown" was neat, with rectilinear streets and, of course, a church. It had an air of prosperity as the traffic from the Potosi silver mines passed through on the way to Spain. The "suburbs" were something else—squatters amidst a jungle of filth and squalor.

Why the have-nots were attracted to the city whereas they might have a healthful, happy life in the countryside where they came from was a mystery—and still is.

Isabel's father, Gaspar de Flores, had been a Spanish soldier, although he was a Puerto Rican with Spanish-born parents. He served under de la Gasca and thus came to Peru to oppose the upstart Gonzalo Pizarro and finally succeeded in deposing the arrogant "governor." With the coming of peace he joined a force going to hostile Inca territory not yet conquered. The going was difficult, the weather fierce, and surprise attacks by the Incas were telling. Even worse, they came to a Spanish captain who claimed that the territory was his by right of possession. Mission accomplished, Flores returned to Lima and became a member of the royal guard. He fell in love with a lovely, well-educated damsel, Maria de Oliva. With parental blessing they were married. They found a huge house with sizable grounds suitable for gardening to provide some income. As the garden grew, so did their family—eight children. They needed all the space in that huge house.

With this scenario it seems improbable that Gaspar would be a likely parent of a saint. The mother, Maria, possibly. But this was the real world and it did happen. Let's see how.

Isabel was number three in that houseful of kids. She must have been special even by the time she was baptized, for the priest added to her certificate: "Hija de estima" (esteemed daughter). She won the love of all. The native maid remarked, "She looks just like a rose." So the babe became known as Rosita—easier to say than Isabel.

As Isabel matured, her adopted name became Rosa. She was special in every way. She read extensively. She ignored the pain of a stubbed toe or a cut finger. Although not antisocial, she preferred quiet and the seclusion of her portion of the garden, which was mostly roses. Moved by church services and with much reading she became enamored of a religious life. She vowed chastity and although she was extremely attractive, she had no interest in suitors.

Her father had been given employment as superintendent of a silver mine in the mountains east of Lima. The family moved there and suffered with inadequate quarters, high altitude, hostile natives, and noxious air that sickened the children. Rosa was ill much of the time and one of her sisters died. Mercury poisoning? Then a series of natural catastrophes occurred—earthquakes, cloudbursts, fires, and tunnel collapses. The mine was closed and the family moved back to their beloved home in Lima.

Rosa was given the opportunity to enter a convent. She decided to stay with her family because she might help support them by sewing and selling garden produce. Too, the family was still growing and needed all hands. She was fourteen.

The third Order of St. Dominic was founded to provide for religious life within the family. Rosa joined and acquired the name of Rosa de Santa Maria. This encouraged her to take in unfortunates and care for them. She overexerted and lost weight. She couldn't sleep. She began to torture herself with self-induced pain. Yet her charges adored her.

Rose acquired the white wool garment of the Dominicans and her work in the infirmary expanded. Two eminent theologians, concerned over her condition, came to talk with her. They were astounded by her mature statements on religion.

Later, when pirates stormed Lima and approached the church to steal artifacts, Rosa hastened there first. As they entered she stood, alone, defiant. Her very bearing intimidated them and they fled.

Rosa's energy failed her, though she was only in her early thirties. Sensing that her end was near, she asked for last rites. News of her death spread rapidly and throngs came to pay respects. She was recognized as the "brightest light ever to shine upon submerged masses of Indians and slaves who made up the larger part of Lima's inhabitants."

Upon receiving word, Pope Urban VIII gave heed and sought supporting testimony. Ultimately, she was canonized. She was recognized as the originator of social service in Peru. She was declared Patroness of Lima and of Peru. And although her remarkable life was nearly four hundred years ago, St. Rose of Lima still lives in the minds of many. Churches are named for her. Prayers recall her blessed name. The goodness that she brought to the world persists.

Now we come to the parallel story of Mariana Paredes y Flores. She was born in Quito, daughter of a Spanish captain of noble birth and a beautiful young lady, also named Mariana, who had been born in Quito.

Not being on the invasion route of the conquistadores, what is now Ecuador had had more peaceful development than its neighbors to the south. Here the Franciscans arrived less than fifty years after the Great Discovery, at about the time Pizarro executed the Inca chieftain, Atahuallpa. Early settlers in Quito had introduced wheat and a wooden plow which the natives quickly adopted. They built a church, established a school, and introduced a culture previously unimagined. Life was fine despite the nine-thousand-foot altitude which made newcomers pant with the slightest exertion. Because of proximity to the equator the climate was mild and the seasons were long.

By the time young Mariana was born there was already a university, a convent, a hospital, a bishop and a thriving community. Mariana's parents had moved in with the maternal family according to custom. Their zest for children was rewarded, for in rapid succession there were eight.

Bearing and delivering child number eight had been difficult and the mother was unable to suckle her baby. So two wet nurses were brought in, one Castilian and one Indian, on the theory that the mixture would be beneficial. Thus our future saint, Marianita, started life. Thriving, she was baptized a month later, November 1618.

Marianita grew up in a religious atmosphere and became highly religious herself. And with early mental maturity she had no difficulty in making decisions—often startling her elders with her audacity. To further her religious training she was given a tutor, Father Camacho. Offered the opportunity to live in a convent, she, like her counterpart, said no. Her choice was to live in the real world where she might directly serve the will of God. She started a service for the poor and ailing. Her dowry had been maintained and she used it to help the poor.

Mariana's self-imposed denial of light, air, space, and nourishment exceeded her strength, but the lines that formed daily at her door increased. She cared for the sick and taught the illiterates. Her successes became legend.

Then the Quito area suffered a series of catastrophes—earthquakes, eruption of volcano Pichincha, pestilences of measles and diptheria. The lives of ten thousand natives and two thousand Spanish were lost. The devastation was so great that the superstitious were sure it signified the wrath of God. In the partly repaired church the priest declared that all this was a retaliation for sin. He called on the people to repent and offered to give his life to save others from the punishment they had brought on themselves. Mariana, without hesitation, arose and announced that she would give her life in lieu of the priest's as he was too much needed in this time of stress. She made a profound impression on the people of Quito.

The strain of all this was too much. She became bedridden and coughed incessantly (undoubtedly she had tuberculosis) and she knew that her end was near. She was only twenty-six.

The bishop, performing the funeral services, fell to his knees silently, then arose, beamed, and proclaimed, "We now have a new advocate in heaven, for Mariana is already there." He then startled the audience by advising that they should not mourn or wear black. Instead, they should celebrate Mariana's contributions to the world by singing praises, bringing flowers, and wearing bright colors. The entire community celebrated.

Years later there was a move for canonization. Again, a study was instigated and the delay seemed endless. Then, with great jubilation in Quito, Santa Mariana was canonized, July 9, 1950. Her sainthood is now recognized worldwide.

Would that we might recognize the contributions of other South American leaders, but to adhere to our pledge of a *brief* narrative we must now go on to other facets of the story. Nor shall we bring the history up to date, as there are many fine references available to the reader. We encourage you to study them.

Chapter 21
Japan Ho! Again

Columbus never delivered the queen's letter of greetings to the Grand Khan of Cipangu, because he and his successors became diverted. Japan wasn't too important anyway, merely the closest Asiatic landfall, according to Marco Polo. Columbus thought he was somewhat south of his intended landfall. All of a sudden Spanish minds were on the New World and gold. There is no record of what happened to that letter.

But the Portuguese, as the greatest seafarers in the world, went in both directions. As we know, they went west, claimed the lands discovered by Columbus, and settled for lands east of the line of demarcation defined by the Treaty of Tordesillas, then went around South America and across the Pacific. They also went east to places like Calcutta, Macao, the Philippines, and Japan. The Spaniards, not wanting to be outdone, soon went west, notably to the Philippines.

By 1580 Spanish friars were getting established in Manila—and this leads to a fascinating saga and the ultimate martyrdom of Friar Pedro Bautista. He, a physically strong young man, eloquent in his Franciscan preaching, inflexibly determined in his convictions, was destined for success. He had a thirst for travel and realized that only by traveling could he bring Christianity to those who needed it. So he volunteered for missionary service in Mexico and a possible transfer to the Philippines. In Mexico he didn't hesitate to visit hostile tribes known for their physical violence. Somehow, Pedro's confident approach and winning personality succeeded in his being welcomed. How different this was from the traditional belligerence of the conquistador!

Pedro's success was recognized, and after three years in Mexico he was selected for transfer to the Philippines and was made a high ranking officer: Comisario Visitador de la Custodio de San Gregorio. This signified that he would be the official representative of at least ten convents. As first assistant he would be in line to become the head of the region.

Pedro sailed from Acapulco, and on his arrival in Manila he and his cohorts were welcomed by the Custodian of San Gregorio. Manila was already a walled city, although it housed only about a hundred families, with Augustinians, Jesuits, and Franciscans vying for position. Pedro's influence would be not only in the city but with the native Tagalogs outside. He soon learned the native language. He also spent much time with a newfound friend, Gonzalo Garcia, another Franciscan, who had spent several years in Japan with Jesuits before he became a Franciscan. Gonzalo knew the Japanese language and was acquainted with several Japanese merchants who resided in Manila.

Pedro offended the governor when he objected to the harsh treatment of the Tagalogs by Spanish soldiers. Not succeeding in his pleading, he spoke out in a sermon. This resulted in the governor's animosity and a public rebuke. A year later the governor was charged with the appointment of an ambassador to Japan. He named Pedro Bautista. Whether this was to get rid of a thorn in his side or in recognition is not clear. Perhaps he heeded the recommendation of Gonzalo García. Probably the latter, for the mission was dangerous, delicate, and highly important to the interests of the Spanish Empire.

Pedro was briefed that the new Togo of Japan was a former worker who had joined the army and risen to the top and then, on the death of the previous Togo, established himself as the new ruler. At this point the Jesuits, who were already well established in Japan, met with hostility. Further teaching of Christianity was prohibited and all missionaries were ordered to depart. This was purely political, for there was no friction with the Buddhists. This would be problem number one for the new ambassador.

Another problem would be the strained relations that had developed between the Portuguese and the Spaniards. The problems were not territorial despite the fact that the Spaniards, under the treaty that they had instigated, were encroaching on Portuguese territory. To go to the Philippines the Spaniards sailed west from the American west coast and the treaty ceded to them everything west of the base meridian. Neither side realized that Philippines are closer to the east of the meridian than to the west. It was not clear what the Jesuits might have done to offend the emperor. Perhaps he knew of the reputation that accompanied the word "Jesuit": a crafty, intriguing, or equivocating person.

On his arrival in Nagasaki mid-1593, the new ambassador was welcomed by the first deputy of the Jesuits. Pedro was invited to a reception but stated that his first obligation was to be received by the "king," as this was necessary protocol. The head of state, who had just adopted the title of Emperor, received him graciously, and Pedro handed over a letter from the Governor of the Philippines. But without even opening the letter the new emperor asserted that the newcomers would do whatever he required of them or he would send his army to Manila—an act which others knew he was already contemplating, along with the seizure of Korea. Pedro, in his first act of diplomacy, soothed the emperor.

Pedro and his party were invited to visit Meaco (Kyoto). Apparently they were expected to stay there, doing nothing. They enjoyed being guests, but Pedro saw the need for missionary work and decided to become active. This would involve travel and although the emperor had given verbal permission for travel throughout Japan, he had no documentation. Nor did it occur to him that Jesuits would give him trouble. He went to Nagasaki and undertook ministry in the hospital. In short time he was visited by a group who told him in no uncertain terms that he and his companions must leave. This time his powers of suasion didn't work. So he wrote to the deputy who had welcomed him to Japan, described the injustice, and insisted that he be free to pursue his own dictates. He pointed out that he was in Japan "with the permission of God, the Pope, King Philip of Spain, the Emperor of Japan, and the Governor of Kyoto!" That didn't work either. Denied even a reply, Pedro and his partner were evicted from the hospital.

Pedro returned to Kyoto and found things running smoothly, though the hospital was overflowing and in need of expansion. Japanese converts and patients were glowing in their expressions of appreciation, stating that never in the history of Japan had such care been provided. A hospital was planned for Osaka, some miles distant.

Then, in 1596, a galleon left Manila, headed for Mexico, with some 250 passengers. The ship's officers didn't know how to read the weather in that part of the world, nor how to respect the force of a typhoon. They were blown across the North China Sea and limped into the port of Urando on the Japanese island of Shikoku. Among the passengers were seven friars. In the hold was a rich cargo of silk which was quickly thrown ashore to avoid deterioration. The galleon sank. A deputation was assembled to go to the Emperor, request a ship to continue the voyage, and for safe storage of the silk until it could be reloaded. En route they stopped in Osaka where Pedro Bautista happened to be visiting. He reassured the group and asked them to thank the emperor for the fine treatment of the shipwrecked Spaniards. Then the ambassador decided to go with them. They were received courteously by the deputy, dined, and told that he would advise when they could have audience with the emperor.

Two days later they received word that the emperor refused to see them. All goods beached from the brigantine were to be confiscated. The soldiers among the passengers were deemed to be a threat to Japan. It was alleged that the ship was engaged in piracy and that the wreck was a hoax. Furthermore, the Portuguese in Japan were not subjects of the Spanish King—providing a clue that the Jesuits may have had a hand in changing the attitude of the emperor. Word hadn't reached them that Philip II had been King of Portugal as well as Spain for fifteen years.

There followed several disagreeable incidents including friction between Jesuit and Franciscan officials. The Jesuit bishop, wanting the expulsion of Franciscan friars and fearing that they would not heed him, sent an emissary to the emperor requesting such an order. The emperor, reversing a previous decision, did issue an order, but it was not for the banishment of the friars. It was for the crucifixion of all Christians! The preaching of Christianity in Japan was intolerable. All priests were to be arrested immediately and guarded.

It was in Kyoto that Pedro Bautista learned the startling, devastating news. The local judge received the order and acted quickly. The friars were arrested and the convent and hospital were without help. Several hundred sympathetic Japanese stormed the premises, overwhelmed the guards, and did their best to restore normalcy. Sensing a more serious portent, Pedro and his associates responded immediately by offering the sacrament of baptism to all who needed it, to hear confessions, and administer communion. Before daybreak the laymen were urged to return to their homes. But more than two hundred stayed, willing to give their lives if necessary. They added their names to the lists of Christians.

In due time the magistrates arrived and read aloud the list of prime offenders—five friars and their staff, including two children. When the name of the carpenter Francisco was called there was no response. He was absent. Immediately the consecrated physician spoke up: "I am Francisco." This group was joined by one from Osaka. Three Jesuits, all Japanese, who had been in the ill-fated shipwreck, were added. Now there were twenty-four. All were handcuffed and marched to the plaza. There the executioner cut off half of the left ear of each one.

From there, they were marched, unprotected, in midwinter, to a seaport. Passing through villages, observers of the solemn death march were moved to tears.

The emperor, not wanting to witness the execution, designated the governor's assistant to perform the spiteful deed. He was known to be hostile to the friars. Waiting for final preparations, he was attracted by the wistful glance of the stalwart little boy, Luisito, and said, "If you would care to come and serve me, I will save you."

Luisito turned to Pedro Bautista and said, "I will do whatever you direct."

Pedro replied, "Tell him you will go to him if he will let you continue life as a Christian." The official shook his head. And the brave Luisito said, "I will remain with my Christian family."

Crosses had arrived and postholes were dug at the usual place of execution at the edge of the city. Friendly natives, going out with food and drink for the prisoners, pleaded that the crosses be placed on the other side of the road where a church might some day be erected. The request was granted.

When the new pits were dug, a cross was placed alongside each and the prisoners were led to their crosses together with three or four executioners for each. Iron rings were affixed to the neck, each wrist and each ankle. These were used instead of spikes because they were not intended to kill but to confine the victims. Then they would be speared to death according to Japanese custom.

Amidst intonations of "Father, forgive them, for they know not what they do," and with the wailings of onlookers, the executioners fulfilled their tasks—first the Japanese, then the lesser friars and, finally, Pedro Bautista. The Calvary was complete.

Gradually Spaniards left Japan. Word of the tragedy reached Spain via Mexico. Another ambassador was sent to Japan—not a Franciscan friar, but a bold captain of infantry. Appearing before the emperor in full uniform he demanded satisfaction for the martyrdom and authority to remove the bodies for decent burial elsewhere. The emperor, impressed by the military presence and authoritative tone of voice, acceded.

Pedro Bautista became the patron of Manila. The number of Christians in Japan increased rapidly. A church was built on the execution site and is there to be visited today.

The pendulum swung again half a century later. Christians were banished. Many death sentences were imposed and carried out before total exile was accomplished.

Admiral Matthew Perry arrived in Japan in 1853 and negotiated a treaty. Trade with America was established. Ports were opened. The clergy returned. And much to their surprise they found that Christianity had somehow survived for two hundred years. Yes, Pedro Bautista made a permanent impact.

Chapter 22
Spain's Ups and Downs

Columbus's historic voyage triggered great excitement in Spain. An influx of untold riches was expected from the conquistadores in the New World. The country developed a renewed self respect and was acquiring new stature. And, in the process, Spain was depleting her meager resources and was diverting her attention from affairs of state closer to home. The Inquisition and the defeat of the Moors had been costly not only in wealth and energy but in talent and culture as well. Half a million of her most valuable countrymen—gone. Queen Isabella, in making supreme effort to straighten out her country, had exhausted herself and shortened her life. She died twelve years after the Great Discovery. King Ferdinand, displaying unexpected genius as he continued the regime, died twelve years later and the baton was passed to Charles I, his grandson, who inherited the country that was teeming with confidence and arrogance. A brilliant future seemed assured. No one surmised that the mighty empire would fail within only a few generations.

Charles I was the son of Philip the Handsome, Archduke of Austria, and Juana the Mad, daughter of Ferdinand and Isabella. He had been raised in the Low Countries, having been born in Ghent. He had been given every educational advantage, specializing in history and preparation for his eventual role as head of state. His instructors were so demanding that he acquired a seriousness which became a characteristic. It was fortunate that his education had been forced, for he became king at age sixteen, though he shared the throne with Juana, his mother. Her role was in title only because of her incapacity. His heritage was excellent despite the mental problems of his mother. And the time in history was propitious from progress as well as foment. So, let's study the life of Charles I in some depth.

While still a youngster Charles had been the unwitting pawn of regal intertwining. Shortly after he was born it was agreed that he should some day marry Claude of France. Relations between France and Spain became strained, however, and the two nations fought. The intended marriage was soon forgotten. In the game of international intrigue and as a stipulation in a treaty with England, Charles was to marry Mary of France, sister of Henry VIII of England. Charles, having reached the ripe old age of fourteen, was deemed old enough to marry and Henry demanded that the marriage take place. But previously King Ferdinand, and Maximilian, the Holy Roman Emperor, had agreed that Charles should be married to the heiress of the crowns of Hungary and Bohemia. They so advised Henry. Immediately, seeing a promising opportunity, Louis XII of France took a fatal step. Though aged and tottering, he asked for the hand of the jilted princess. His nuptials hastened his end and Mary was a widow almost as soon as she was a bride. Eventually, Charles married Eleonora, daughter of the King of Portugal.

Although Charles had established a residence in Spain, management of that country was entrusted to the celebrated Cardinal Ximenes. That was not to last, however, for Maximilian died and Charles I added the title of Charles V, Emperor of the Holy Roman Empire. This necessitated his leaving Spain to take possession of his new domain. At the same time he received word that Cortes was making headway with his campaign in Mexico. Now Charles I/V owned Spain, which included Castile, Aragon, and Granada. He was King of Naples and Sicily and Duke of Milan. He was lord of Franche-Comte and of the Low Countries. He was titular King of England. He possessed the Cape Verde Islands and the Canaries and much of the North Coast of Africa, as represented by Tunis and Oran. He owned the Philippines, the Spice Islands, Mexico, and Peru. No other ruler in history had inherited such a vast responsibility. No wonder he was sobersided and worried.

The Spanish were displeased at the outset of Charles's reign by his maintaining a Flemish Court while attempting to impose ironclad rule and increased taxes in Spain. This wasn't Charles's personal doing, however, but that of the cardinal. Towns developed vigilantes and revolted, but fortunately, the uprising was soon crushed after a few executions.

Then Germany demanded all of Charles's attention. Religious uprisings were occurring, especially at the instigation of Martin Luther, who sought religious liberty. He had taken issue with Dominican teachings, had developed a list of ninety-five differences with their creed, and was labeled as a radical. Charles attempted to reconcile the differences and convened a conference attended by Luther with security provided by the emperor. Controversy spread, however, and Luther appealed to Charles for assistance. Dissention spread through Germany. Luther, not to be sidetracked, contended that the Pope had no right to interpret the Bible any more than any other person. He and his cohorts were excommunicated. But Lutheranism was under way and would continue. The emperor, seeking moderation against the Protestants, tried to remain silent. But as defender of the Roman Catholic Church he found it necessary to issue a rebuke to Martin Luther.

Emperor Charles V's power was so vast that other European princes became envious and uneasy. The principal states of Italy leagued together and selected Pope Clement VII to oppose him. So, the Constable of Bourbon besieged Rome, took the city, sacked it, and took the Pope prisoner. Again embarrassed, Charles had to publicly rebuke the Constable. Wearing so many hats must have been insufferable.

Because of polarization, Henry VIII of England allied with the French monarch against Charles. Along came another war. This one concluded in 1529 by the Treaty of Cambray. It was favorable to Charles.

Charles's friendliness toward the Protestants paid dividends when he contended with the Turks. The Ottoman Empire, headquartered in Constantinople, was menacing Mediterranean traffic. Protestants hastened to support the cause against Emperor Suleiman. In a battle of the Cross vs. the Crescent, the Turks were defeated. In an expedition against Tunis some two hundred thousand slaves were released. Thus Charles's stature in Christendom was high. Later, visiting Martin Luther's grave, he stated, "I do not war with the dead. Let him rest in peace. He is already before his Judge."

Then things started going downhill for Charles. His plan for uniting all religious parties was futile. The Tyrol revolted. The Council of Trent was dissolved. He lost Lorraine. He lost Siena. Hard-pressed by his enemies, dejected over no longer being supreme, and feeling that his motives had been misunderstood, he became disheartened and withdrew from public life. It seemed time to transfer the rule to his son, Philip. He convened a council that heard his case and agreed. Philip, now nearly thirty, was ready. He had already ruled Castile. He had the distinction of having a chain of islands named for him—the Philippines—by the navigator, Villelobos.

This anecdote dates back to King Ferdinand, who was concerned over the inroads of the Portuguese who had started trading in Asiatic spices. Ferdinand had counselled with his ablest navigators and explorers, searching for a way to outmaneuver his Portuguese neighbors. Even Hernan Cortes, conqueror of Mexico, volunteered to become a seafarer. But it was Villelobos who crossed the Pacific, found his way to the beautiful harbor that would become Manila, and laid claim.

Elaborate preparations were made for the transfer of power from Charles to Philip, in the Great Hall in Brussels. The procession was both colorful and historic. The ceremony was brief. Charles capsulized his career and relieved his mind of any thought that he had done less than his best. He gave a full vote of confidence to his son's ability. Thus ended a most remarkable regime: international contention; competing religions; piracy on the high seas; progress in the New World; and Spain, withal, had become a world power. All this could not have occurred without the expenditure of tremendous wealth—wealth from the New World. Expenditures were equal to or greater than income, as if the influx of gold and silver would continue forever. One can wonder whether all that wealth acquired with cruelty and the expenditure of lives really made for a better world. But in

Spain it did set the stage for a higher morality, improved education, and stimulated writing, music, and the theatre. Too bad Queen Isabella could not have stayed alive to witness the rewards of the rebirth that she initiated.

Fortunately, Philip II could afford his costly galaxy of nations. Riches still arrived from the New World, particularly silver. No one since Caesar, if then, had held more authority. But scholars began to speculate as to how long so much might could remain with one man.

Philip's power was temporal. The Pope's was spiritual. And here a split developed, despite the fact that Philip considered himself an ally of the papacy and loyal to its incumbent, Paul IV. Paul had been a cardinal, close to Philip, before becoming Pope.

Paul's Caraffa family had long disliked the rulers of Aragon and therefore opposed its King Ferdinand and his rule of the Kingdom of Naples. They maintained that Naples had been siezed unfairly and that it should rightfully be governed by the Pope. So when Cardinal Caraffa was appointed Archbishop of Naples, Charles had to oppose the appointment. And when the cardinal became Pope, he took his prejudices with him. He appointed unqualified members of his family to high positions, such as naming a soldier nephew as the new cardinal. He played footsy with France and even arranged a secret treaty providing for troops and financing to help recover Naples. Charles learned of this and reversed the situation, buying his way with bankrupt France.

The new cardinal maintained dialog with the French ruler and when Charles retired pointed out that the inexperienced son was weak. If Henry of France would reverse himself and support the Pope, he could name members of his family to rule Naples and Milan. The gullible

Henry fell for it and another treaty was signed. It seems that treaties were a dime a dozen, hardly worth the cost of the paper.

Now it was Philip's turn again and this time he was more prudent. He had the Church itself adopt a case against the Pope, favoring a defensive war. The Pope added to his defense by hiring some German mercenaries who followed wars as a profession and were always available to the highest bidder. In the fracas Rome itself was threatened. The Pope and the French were defeated.

Philip may have wanted peace but such was not his destiny. Nor was he destined for a long-lasting marital life. Before becoming emperor he had married Mary of England, but abandoned her and her country "because of the weather." Then he wooed her sister, Elizabeth, but learned that they had serious political differences, primarily religious: Catholicism vs. Protestantism. Mary, Queen of Scots, was a devoted French Catholic who had an ambition to control the English throne. During a turmoil she fled to England for security but instead was imprisoned by Queen Elizabeth who was sure that Mary had become too much of a risk for English Protestantism. When a conspiracy arose, Elizabeth feared the worst and ordered the beheading of Mary, Queen of Scots. Mary, still feeling she was right, uttered her final prayer, in Latin: "O Domini Deus, speravi in te. O care mi Jesu. . . ." This was the end of Catholicism in England. And Philip, the Catholic, breathed a sigh of relief that he had not married Elizabeth.

So, instead of marrying Elizabeth, Philip married Isabella, daughter of Henry II of France. Unfortunately, she died eleven years later, and in the same year Philip married his niece, Anne of Austria. Nor did she survive him. Confusing? Imagine the confusion in royal circles, trying to keep track of offspring and family ties. The family tree must have looked like a bramble patch.

As if to fulfill the dreams of Columbus, the Spaniards finally, after about seventy-five years of trial and error, established a foothold in the Far East and were trading in copra and coconut-shell products, cottons, burlap, rope, and filigree jewelry. Manila had been founded in 1571. Filipinos were being Christianized. Trade had been initiated with the Chinese. The Chinese liked the relationship so well that they almost overpopulated Manila. Chinese silks were all the rage in Europe and were always in short supply, primarily because of transportation bottlenecks.

To get to the Philippines, ships crossed the Atlantic to Vera Cruz, Mexico. Thence a hazardous land crossing to Acapulco. By barge to galleons at anchor, for Acapulco had no deep water. From there would be nine thousand miles of open ocean requiring at least sixty days.

The return trip was even more arduous, for it was necessary to find northbound and eastbound winds and currents. Magellan of Portugal wasn't lucky, gave up, and was killed by natives. His ship had to go the other way around the world and was the first to circumnavigate the globe. By accident, the captain of a Spanish galleon found the winning route: go north, pick up the Japanese Kuroshio current, follow the winds and currents and migratory seabirds around to the California coast, and thence south to Acapulco. This took about seven months. Depending on weather, some completed it faster. Others became becalmed, ran out of water and food, and perished. Interestingly, the eastbound trip was the same as described by Heyerdahl for the pre-Incans.

Just as Philip's immediate family experienced misfortune, his empire, too, began to decline—with oppression, religious intolerance, war, insurrections. Loss of the Netherlands because of religious differences. German Protestants warring against Ghent and Pope Clement VIII. Expenditures in excess of income despite the tremendous wealth flowing in from the Western Hemisphere. Philip had to borrow. He had lost a million soldiers. His great monarchy began to decline, though the arts flourished. Philip II died in 1598 at the age of seventy-one. Despite all well-intended preparations, his son, Philip III, was far from capable. He lost territory, suffered from inroads of Protestantism, and his domain continued to decline.

Philip III was worried over the Moslems who had remained in Spain, including those who had intermarried with Spaniards. Threatened with rebellion, he expelled them all—some six hundred thousand. This depopulated some areas and disrupted farming and trade. He warred with Germany, Italy, Netherlands, and France. Spain developed factions internally, and Portugal separated. In all, Philip III lost three million citizens. Had he planned to dismember his empire he couldn't have done better. His successors, Philip IV and Philip V, failed. Thus, Spain wallowed in contention until nearly 1800.

Chapter 23
The Land of Everything

What land has everything? Tahiti? Switzerland? New Zealand? Try South America. More particularly, Incaland: Peru, Ecuador, most of Chile, part of Bolivia, a bit of Colombia, and parts of the rain forests of what is now Brazil. Accustomed to looking at maps in atlases, we tend to think of such areas as being flat. Too bad those atlases don't have three-dimensional relief maps, for South America has the largest mountain chain of any continent.

The mineral-rich Andes extend for forty-five hundred miles, from the Caribbean to Cape Horn. They boast forty-five peaks higher than twenty thousand feet. North America has one (Denali, Alaska). The Andes comprise three chains (cordilleras), roughly parallel ridges which provide distinctive climates in the belts between. The Inca civilization flourished in the region between the central and eastern chains, the Sierras. Geologists tell us how this spectacular wrinkle of the earth's surface happened to occur. The answer lies in the behavior of tectonic plates.

Some two billion years ago all the continents were

bunched together in what is now the South Atlantic. They fitted together neatly. For instance, the coasts of Africa and South America almost match. The continents (let's now think of them as plates) gradually separated and drifted, like rafts, on the molten core of the earth. They continue to move, some as rapidly as they ever did—*very* slowly.

When the westerly (Nazca) plate which lies under the Pacific Ocean met another (South American) plate, it was forced to keep moving. It went under, causing the other to uplift. Thus, mountain ranges in South America. The force to uplift a row of 20,000-foot peaks is beyond normal comprehension. Nature has its way.

Tectonic uplift caused cracks (faults) in the earth's crust, some deep enough to permit molten lava to erupt. Several South American volcanoes continue to be active. The uplift also tilted the eastern portion of the continent, providing the gentle slope just right for river flow—over two million square miles of the Amazon drainage area and its rain forests. South America engages in huge numbers. The Amazon's length is about four thousand miles.

Movement of tectonic plates continues. The typical rate is about two inches per year, comparable to the rate of growth of a toenail—you can't see it happening. But, for plates, the rate may not be uniform. Due to irregularities along fault lines, the sides may get bound up until the force exceeds the resistance. Then it lets go with an unexpected jerk—an earthquake. The natives attributed earthquakes to the supernatural, the vengeance of the gods.

The molten core of the earth has a concentration of exotic minerals, some of which have found their way to the surface through faults or volcanoes. Thus gold is found the full length of the Andes. In fact, some twenty-five minerals are found there. We discuss gold in another chapter. Silver became as important as gold. A saddle connects the central and eastern cordilleras and is the site of the celebrated Cerro de Pasco silver mine.

Mountain ranges have another role. They affect weather. Westbound moisture-laden air is trapped by the Andes and spills its cargo over the rain forests. On the Pacific side of the Andes lies a coastal shelf that receives virtually no rain at all. Lifeless desert, it reminds one of the surface of the moon. That coastal fringe is over a hundred miles wide and extends nearly fifteen hundred miles north-south. The Atacama Desert in northern Chile is itself six hundred miles long. With fertile soil and decent climate other than rain, it challenged natives to tap rivers, develop irrigation, and grow bountiful crops at sea level. They needed fertilizer and gathered the droppings of the myriads of birds that dove for anchovies in the warm ocean current just offshore. Those droppings, guano, were ideal fertilizer and they used a large amount. But they didn't exhaust the supply. It was 150 feet thick in some places.

It is almost embarrassing to use so many superlatives, yet they are warranted. Between the two main cordilleras lies one of the most remarkable lakes on the globe—Lake Titicaca. It is huge—130 miles long and 30 miles wide, though in one area it is wider. Its surface lies at the breathtaking altitude of 12,635 feet. Despite its high altitude it attracted prehistoric people. One of its islands gave birth to the Inca legend.

This book is not intended to be a travelogue, but the location of Lake Titicaca should be identified. It is several hours southeast of Cuzco by rail, a fascinating trip through the Altaplana. It is a hundred miles north of La

Paz, easily reached by bus. And it is close to heaven. The lake and its shore continues to support many natives, wearing colorful homespuns. The reeds growing in shallow areas are made into those unique reed boats. It is startling to see a heavyset "Indian" woman wearing a brown derby hat paddling along in her reed boat.

The equator crosses the middle of Ecuador (hence the name). We think of equatorial latitudes as being tropical. Here, due to its high altitudes, it freezes, right on the equator.

Beautiful, historic Incaland is a geologic wonder and a region of unparalleled archaelogic treasures. The natives did appreciate their world and also were in awe of it. They were frequently reminded of the workings of their gods—in the form of earthquakes, thunderstorms, avalanches, and eclipses. But their god, the sun, was only spiteful on occasion. He gave them a wonderful land and passed over them every day, keeping an eye on them.

Unfortunately, tourism in South America hasn't developed for providing access to some of the most interesting places, like the giant quarry and the hot springs at Cajamarca. Nor are many tourists comfortable at extremely high altitudes. Even the Pan American Highway is too much of a challenge for most. But many wonders are readily accessible. Among the most exciting places I have visited are:

●Quito (gold museum)
●San Agustin, Colombia (prehistoric statues)
●Cuzco
●Machu Picchu (stay overnite & see the sunrise)
●La Paz (and the carnival at Oruru)
●Lima
●Iquitos (Upper Amazon)

- Canyon Diablo, en route to Cerro de Pasco)
- Nazca Desert and intaglios
- Santiago (and those paintings in the Cathedral)
- Rio de Janeiro
- Chilean fjords and glaciers
- Chilean lakes
- Iguazu Falls
- Cape Horn Island
- Patagonia

If you haven't "done" them, it's time to start making plans.

Chapter 24
What If——

Balboa assembled two brigantines on the Pacific side of the Isthmus of Panama and had the parts for two more. He certainly must have felt certain that he could, if he so chose, sail on to the Spice Islands to fulfill Columbus's dream. If so, he must have decided that the prospect of obtaining gold was more important. What if he had decided otherwise? Would he have reached Japan, Ceylon, or some place on the Asiatic coast? Would this have changed the history of the world as dramatically as what actually happened? And how would he have returned to Spain?

Balboa would have had no better information than Columbus as to the distance across the Pacific. He probably would have sailed with insufficient supplies for such a long voyage, resulting in starvation, mutiny, or vulnerability to storms. Japan and Spain have about the same latitude. Panama and the Philippines are about the same. But had he traveled that far, he would come to other traffic and could establish communication.

Had Balboa succeeded in crossing the Pacific, establishing a new trade route would have been as difficult as pioneering the old Silk Road—unless he mustered enough navigational daring to attempt a return via the Indian Ocean, around the Cape of Good Hope, and up the west coast of Africa. Rather iffy.

Another conjecture—what if Balboa instead of Pizarro had led the expedition to Incaland? Balboa's strategy was to make friends with the natives. Pizarro's was brutal conquest. Save for the chicanery that eliminated him, Balboa would have been the likely leader to head the expedition southward, with a probability that Pizarro would have been a member of the party.

Would Balboa have enlisted the Incas into some sort of partnership? A working coalition? Together they might have forged one of the mightiest territories of the world. The Spaniards could contribute what the Incas didn't have—a written language, the wheel, vehicles, horses, steel tools and weapons, armed might to resist aggressors, ships to sail the Pacific, Christianity, and a culture based on thousands of years of civilization. The Incas could have contributed gold and silver, agricultural products to help feed a destitute part of Europe, an all-inclusive social security system, and a whole new world insofar as Europeans were concerned.

The Peruvians had probably navigated the Amazon to its mouth at the Atlantic. From what became Belem to Cadiz would have been a pushover, much shorter than from Panama.

Wheeled vehicles would have required a new highway system. Schools and churches would have proliferated. And no doubt urbanization would have kept pace. Internal conflicts would have been inevitable. Would they have had the wisdom to negotiate them? But overall the world might have developed more rapidly than it actually did, with less anguish, fewer lives lost, and closer approach to the principles of Queen Isabella.

Spain would have had to grant some sort of autonomy to its enterprise in the Western Hemisphere. It took eight months to send a message from Castile to Peru and an equal time for a return message—an impossible situation. Total delegation of authority to a trusted person (if there was one) would have been the obvious answer.

Would such a development have changed political and economic Europe? Yes. But it probably would have changed the regal rat race, the quest for power, planned intermarriages, and attempts to dominate. Any of these might have resulted in conflict. Or it might have resulted in the emergence of a world leader, the like of whom the world had seldom seen.

One can ask, "Did the Pope have a right to cede lands to Spain and Portugal? Didn't he realize he was expropriating the property of the rightful owners? Wouldn't he have been wiser to establish protectorates, making the 'conquerors' responsible for the welfare of the natives?" The Pope obviously believed that the heathens had no rights. It is also obvious that the natives were ignorant of Christianity—but ignorance is no reason for having one's land seized. Should he not have first tried to convert them? Would they then have become Spanish and Portuguese citizens with rights? The quest for gold overwhelmed any such considerations. Christianity could come later.

The question persists: What if ——?

Chapter 25

Those Paintings

Diego Almagro was anxious to get away from his contentious partner, Francisco Pizarro. There was interest in exploring farther south from the area that is known as Lima, Peru. How refreshing might it be, thought Diego, to avoid the daily bickering and venture out with a small party of soldiers. The expedition was arranged and Almagro even took along the interpreter, Felipillo. This was a futile gesture, for native tribes had developed different languages and had trouble communicating with each other. However, with little difficulty, Almagro ventured as far south as the present Santiago, Chile. He returned to rejoin the despicable Pizarro, and to bring a favorable report for future colonization.

A follow-up expedition was led by Pedro de Valdevia, a latecomer to the Western Hemisphere. He was not only an able military officer but a devout Catholic. He soon won the respect of Francisco Pizarro and was entrusted with the responsibility of leading a colonizing party. Valdevia was a good choice, for some armed resistance had developed and he soon overcame it. He went on to found the "Colonia del Nuevo Extremo" (Colony of the New Extreme), on February 12, 1541. It is now Santiago, Chile.

Let's go back for a moment and try to decipher what happened when Valdevia met armed resistance. According to one legend, the Incas, led by their princess, La Ñusta Huillac, resolved to resist any trespassing into their territory. The princess was so defiant that she became known as La Tirana (the tyrant). She and her warriors captured a member of Valdevia's party, a Portuguese, Vasco de Almeyda. According to their tradition, they condemned him to death. But when La Ñusta had the prisoner brought to her, she was so impressed with his attractiveness and his stories of his country and his people, she wanted to know more. The execution was deferred, then canceled, for they fell in love. The Inca priests were furious when they discovered Vasco baptizing the beautiful princess. Both were sentenced to death. La Ñusta reminded her judges that she was the last of the Inca princesses and was priestess of the cult of the sun. She asked that she be buried with her beloved husband and that a cross be placed over the grave. Her wish was fulfilled and years later when Christianity came to that land, a church was erected at the site and tradition grew.

Today, the small town of La Tirana, in the north of Chile, about fifty miles inland from the coastal town of Iquique, is the center of an annual pilgrimage. For three days, July 14–16, thousands of pilgrims congregate in La Tirana, near the village church. As many as thirty

thousand return year after year. The festival is strongly religious, a composite of pagan and Christian rites. Costumes are colorful and richly decorated, differing among various communities. They also bring their own music and individualistic dances and try to outperform each other. They sing in front of the statue of Christ, enter the church to worship the Virgin, then proceed to the town square for more performances. Though some performers fall asleep, activity is continuous, day and night, for three days when, finally, the climax is reached: the Virgin is carried through the multitude, bells and all manner of instruments are drowned out by voices. When the Virgin reenters the church, costumes are shed, tearful good-byes are said, and the long journeys home are undertaken, with a resolve to repeat the ritual the following year.

A similar carnival is held annually in Oruro, Bolivia, a mining town not far from La Tirana. I was once privileged to witness its parade. In the parade, leading citizens displayed their treasures on the hoods of their cars, even to extent of sterling silver tableware. The miners union marched to the chant of singers. Devil dancers wove in and out of the procession. The architects and engineers union, in pagan costume, was spectacular. If it were ever to enter the Tournament of Roses Parade, it would steal the show.

Now, back to Valdevia. In preparing for his expedition, Valdevia had carefully hollowed out his saddle bow and concealed in it a beautifully carved statuette of the Virgin. He promised himself that should his venture be successful, he would build a sanctuary at the "Extremo" with the Virgin having a place of prominence. And when his soldiers dispersed the native challengers with cavalry charges and shouts of "Santiago," he blessed the Virgin for their easy victory.

The battle cry "Santiago" (St. James) was traditional

with Spaniards. It stemmed from the heroic life of the saint who was buried in one of Spain's most revered sites, Santiago-de-Compostella. The name "Santiago" has been anglicized as "San Diego." To Valdevia it seemed appropriate to name the new colony Santiago.

For two years or so the new colony stalled and appeared to have an uncertain future, despite the fact that the Virgin had been declared the patroness and had been placed in Valdevia's hermitage.

After about twenty-five years, the hermitage was dilapidated and somewhat isolated. The thriving little city was ready for a cathedral, centrally located, with towers rising high above its surroundings. A magnificent structure was planned and construction was started in 1568. What to name it? The Franciscans proposed that it should commemorate the founder of their order, the brother of trees and animals, the inspiration for missionary efforts, St. Francis of Assisi. Thus, the Catedral de San Francisco (Cathedral of St. Francis) was established.

The design of the church was so ambitious that construction required twenty-seven years, though chapels were completed quickly and the Virgin always had a place of prominence.

The life of Francis of Assisi was well known and carefully documented. Assisi, his birthplace, is in a mountainous area inland and north of Rome and thus is near the center of Catholicism. His parents were wealthy. His father, who, incidentally, had his son baptized "John," was overbearing and overly ambitious.

When old enough for military duty John served, became a prisoner of war, and was seriously ill. Religion had begun to dominate over everything else. When free, he calmly changed his entire life. He "resigned" from his domineering father and even changed his name from John to Francis. His new life was one of deliberate poverty—even begging for food in order to survive. His income from the family fortune was spent on restoration of churches where he worked as a laborer. Some thought he was a madman when he preached the necessity of penance. Gradually, however, his views gained support and the "Preachers of Penance" was founded and was given papal approval. This became the Friars Minor—the Franciscan Order. The Franciscans have continued for some eight hundred years, are established worldwide, and are honored for their missionary efforts. And Francis of Assisi was sainted.

Assisi has changed slightly: A basilica was built, honoring the great St. Francis. I recall visiting there and being impressed with a beautiful marble statue of St. Francis in the courtyard. It seemed most suitable that the sculptor had placed a white dove on the shoulder of this lover of birds and animals. The light was just right for a picture. As the shutter clicked, the dove flew away! But my picture includes the dove.

Notable Italian artists have contributed paintings. Above the altar are paintings depicting Poverty, Chastity, Obedience, and the Triumph of St. Francis. In the upper basilica, the great Giotto has frescoed some twenty-eight scenes of the life of the Saint—and these relate to the paintings in the museum of the Catedral de San Francisco, Santiago, Chile.

The museum of the cathedral houses an invaluable collection of fifty-four colonial paintings of episodes in the life of St. Francis. They are large, averaging more than six feet by nine feet. They are the work of accomplished artists, which gave rise to my quest to know who and where and when. Although I have seen the paintings and photographed some of them, the search for facts has been one of the most elusive challenges in my research for this book. I went down many blind alleys to no avail. Finally, a plausible explanation emerged and although it is not precise, it is believable, for a variety of bits of evidence dovetail together. Although the following description appears to be factual, it is really a recital of best available evidence.

The paintings were executed during a sixteen-year period, 1668–1684. They are the work of at least four artists, including two Americans (half-breeds) and two Europeans, although one of the latter might have been an American who was trained in Europe. One of the Americans was named Juan Zapaca Inga. All were of the same school of interpretation and technique. The fifty-four episodes were carefully selected and composed. The groupings of figures, brushstrokes, and colors show European influence, yet they include Western Hemisphere influences. Backgrounds are native, as are component parts of clothing, jewelry, fruits, flowers, and household objects—all characteristic of seventeenth century Peruvian and Chilean culture.

The Church of St. Francis in Cuzco has a series of thirty canvases of the life of St. Francis. It is probable that the Santiago paintings were produced there also, then sent to Santiago on llamas over Inca highways. The pictorial records of the life of the saint are those that were popular in Spain and Portugal. Knowledge of such traditions would have reached Cuzco early during the Spanish conquest, thanks to an influx of Franciscans and Jesuits. Although the military aspects of the crusade were not conducive to art, a Cuzco art school, the Basilio de Santa Cruz, did exist. One native-born artist, half-breed Juan Christómo Inga, was both a painter and sculptor. Paintings in both Cuzco and Santiago bear the signature of a Zapaca Inga.

A study of the Santiago paintings discloses a close parallel between the life of Christ and that of St. Francis. They are a combination of the dramatic and the picturesque, typical of colonial works. There is every evidence of painstaking preparation and meticulous selection of colors. One commentator observes, "A restrained emotion, remindful of El Greco, exudes from the entire series." Yes, they are excellent.

Take, for example, Painting No. 5, showing Francis inclined to sainthood at an early age. "At a sumptuous banquet in the paternal mansion, rising from the table, he takes his plate and daily bread and proffers them to a beggar. The supper is painted in lively colors. The guests are richly attired in velvets and fine laces. The ladies wear pearls. . . . On a table covered with whitest linen stand some dishes with choice morsels of chicken, some brown loaves, a sweet dish and some exquisite-appearing fruit and vegetables—lemons, peppers, paprika, peaches, apples, pears, grapes, pomegranate. The child is in gala dress—velvet quilter, silken hose, beribboned footwear. The beggar wears broken sandals."

The paintings have survived earthquakes but weren't there for the devastating one in 1647 which destroyed Santiago except for the cathedral. Builders had ingeniously tied together the masonry walls and roof timbers—perhaps the first example of successful earthquake engineering. The tower, however, fell. Fortunately, it missed the Virgin.

The surfaces of the paintings did suffer the ravages of time, so, after three hundred years, they were restored by an artist, Ramon Campos, who completed his work in 1975. A new museum was built in 1982 to house this most valuable collection.

It is my hope that these paintings can someday go on tour, to become featured exhibits in U.S. art museums, so that they can be appreciated by a wide audience. I will try to help bring this about.

Chapter 26

Nazca

When Almagro and, later, Valdevia, went southward from Lima, each was seeking sites for possible settlement. They also scouted for native tribes which might be friendly or hostile, probably the latter. Thus it is likely that they didn't pause to admire the beauties of nature or appreciate features that would excite an archaeologist or a geologist. Following Inca roads and coming to the Nazca desert about ten days below Lima, they undoubtedly hastened across, hoping that they wouldn't run out of water. Certainly they were unaware that they were in the midst of the world's most unique astronomical display.

Stretching across the desert are straight lines, miles

long, scratched into the desert varnish-covered stony surface. Among them are huge figures of birds and animals and various geometric figures. To see them clearly one should hover over them at an altitude of a thousand feet or so. To create them without soaring to the same height would tax the mathematical ingenuity of an advanced people. There is no record, only conjecture, as to how or why these lines and figures were created. Without knowing they were there a traveler might go through, totally unaware of their existence. In fact, it was not until 1939 that they were discovered. By 1946, Maria Reiche, a German mathematician and geographer, became intrigued with the challenge of studying them.

Maria moved to the Nazca Desert and devoted the balance of her life to the study. We had a fascinating visit with her early in 1977. Thirty years of single-purpose study had not dimmed her enthusiasm for her unique subject. She was most generous in discussing her findings and her theories.

Ancient Peruvians and Bolivians observed heavenly bodies and fixed important dates, as evidenced by various ruins and stone structures. These were as sophisticated as those of Stonehenge and elsewhere in southern Britain or the Egyptian pyramids or the intaglios of the western deserts, or in the Southeast of the United States. Maria was aware of these, as well as the remarkable structures at Cuzco and Machu Pichu, before she learned of the Nazca Intihuatanas (the places where the sun is tied). So, to her, it was a privilege to study "the most important astronomical monument in Peru, and perhaps of the world."

Maria soon enlisted the support of the Peruvian air force. A north-south area thirty miles long was photographed from positions as nearly vertical as possible. Prints disclosed an amazing array of lines and figures, unbelievably precise and mostly, or perhaps all, interrelated. Maria had her challenge to decipher the vast array of lines, triangles, rectangles, trapezoids, whorls, circles; and outlines of birds, animals, and mysterious creatures.

The pampas, barren flat land, was ideal for this "communication with the gods." With negligible rainfall and runoff, every rock had remained undisturbed since time immemorial. Desert varnish, the discoloration of exposed surfaces of rocks under the intense sunlight contrasted with natural color of the underlay, thus giving the works virtual permanence.

In searching for clues, Maria and a Dr. Paul Kosok first studied two parallel lines. One was 2,600 feet long. This happened to be on June 21, summer solstice, and they happened to be at a vantage point when the sun set. Surely enough, the sun was aligned—almost. Calculations showed that there would have been perfect alignment between A.D. 350 and 950. With this encouragement they studied other lines and found one which aligned with the setting sun on December 21, winter solstice, some time between the first and sixth century B.C. Recording the longest and shortest days of the year has been important to several cultures worldwide. That early Peruvians understood and recorded these phenomena is testimony to their sophistication. That they were willing to move thousands of tons of rock to build their observatory is testimony to their devotion.

It began to be apparent that other lines must have recorded the positions where other heavenly bodies set and rose. Dr. Kosok named them "the largest astronomy book in the world." He conjectured that if there was a belief that heavenly bodies were responsible for the destinies of men and nations (witness the Inca belief in their emergence from th sun and moon), then surely they influenced a way of thinking. Their attempted communication by means of gigantic figures was thus plausible.

Sensationalists were quick to fantasize that the Nazca lines were the landing field for creatures from outer space. One even contended that he had seen a space ship and its occupants. This made for best-selling science fiction. But what the authors didn't realize is that, in this instance, truth is stranger than fiction.

Reiche and Kosok began studying gigantic birds, monkeys, a canine-like figure, spiders, and lizards. One bird with a snakelike neck has a bill extending in a solstice direction, thus demonstrating a relationship between figures and astronomical directions. This bird is more than 700 feet long.

A spider, 150 feet long, is integrated with a series of straight lines. They placed it on the agenda for future study. Likewise, two huge trapezoids about 2,400 feet long awaited explanation. A monkey, leaning forward and extending expressive hands, has an enormous tail wrapped into a spiral having five concentric rings. It is an outline drawing which might be completed with one continuous "pencil line." Over 300 feet wide, it is interconnected with a geometric figure.

Measurements in several places disclose increments in ratios of ten and one hundred, another proof that early Peruvians understood the decimal system. This provided a clue that the translation from a scale drawing to ground might have been by a factor of one hundred. For precise layout of curved portions of a figure the builders resorted to arcs and circles easily traced by stretching a line from a center.

Maria Reiche told us of another clue to the sophisticated civilization of early Peruvians—weaving. An unknown people called Paracas inhabited the southern desert near the Nazca site, and excelled in weaving, perhaps as early as 400 B.C. Their neighbors, the Mochicas, were equally skilled. They used a backstrap loom, a portable device, one end of which was tied to a tree or wall. The other end had a rope which went around the weaver so that, by leaning, getting just the right tautness was easy. Alpaca, llama, and vicuna wool was used. Vicuna, the world's finest, was almost like silk. Later, when trade was established, cotton was a favorite fabric.

Dyeing was another achievement, with colors in all hues. Their purple came from a shell-fish, comparable to the murex in the Mediterranean. Spinning on a hand-held spindle was just like that of Egypt as early as 3,000 B.C.

Fortunately, the practice of attiring a deceased person in fine raiment has provided many examples of superior craftmanship. Their tombs were excellent preservation chambers.

Maria's only regret was she would not live long enough to decipher the amazing culture of the predecessors of the Incas—artisans, astronomers, mathematicians, inventors, spiritualists, and likely much more than we now know.

Bibliography

Acosta, Jose de. *The Naturall & Morall Histore of the East and West Indies*. London: Hakluyt Soc., 1604.

Anderson, Charles Loftus Grant, *Life & Letters of Vasco Núñez de Balboa*. New York: Revelle Co., 1941.

Archaeology Magazine. "Rediscovering the Inca Heritage." 1985.

Beltran, Miriam. *Cuzco, Window on Peru*. New York: Knopf, 1970.

Bennett, Wendell C. *Ancient Arts of the Andes*. New York: Museum of Modern Art, 1954.

Bingham, Hiram. *Lost City of the Incas*. New York: Duell, Sloan, and Pearce, 1922, 1948.

——. *Inca Land*. Boston and New York: Houghton Mifflin, 1922.

——. *Machu Picchu*. Madrid: Ediciones Zig-Zag. 1949.

Birney, Hoffman. *Brothers of Doom* (Pizarros). New York: G.P. Putnam and Sons, 1942.

Bray, Warwick. *The Gold of El Dorado*. London: Times Newspapers Ltd., 1978.

Brundage, Burr C. *Lords of Cuzco*. Norman: University of Oklahoma Press, 1985.

Bushnell, G. H. S., *Peru*. New York: Praeger, 1957.

Cervantes Saavedra, Miguel de. *Don Quixote*. New York: Knopf, 1960.

Cieza de Leon, Pedro de. *Chronicle of Peru, Civil Wars of Peru, The Travels of P. de C. de L*. Norman: University of Oklahoma Press, 1959.

Cobo, Father Bernabe. *Historia del Nuevo Mundo*. Austin, Universty of Texas Press, 1979.

Columbus, Christopher. Collection of autographed letters, signed, his book of privileges and original papers of the King and Queen. London: Maggs Bros., London, 1923, 1928.

———. *From Panama to Peru*. London: Maggs Bros., 1936.

———. The first extant letter from America. London: Maggs Bros., London, N.d.

Cortes Society. *Documents & Narratives concerning the Discovery and Conquest*. Berkeley: University of California Press, N.d.

Darwin, Charles. *The Voyage of the Beagle*. New York: Doubleday, 1962.

de Zarate, Augustin et al. *The Discovery and Conquest of Peru*. N.p., n.d.

Dickerson, John. *Pottery Making, A Complete Guide*. New York: Viking Press, 1974.

Dobyns, Henry E. & Doughty, Paul L. *Peru—A Cultural History*. Oxford: Oxford University Press, 1976.

Eckhart & Griffith. *Temples in the Wilderness*. Tucson: Arizona Historical Society, 1975.

Elliott, J. H. *Imperial Spain 1469–1716*. New York: St. Martin Press, 1963.

Encyclopedia Americana

Encyclopedia Britannica

Erickson, Johnathan, E. *Peopling of the New World*. Los Altos: Ballena Press, 1982.

Flournoy, Bertrand. *The World of the Incas*. New York: Vanguard, 1956.

Frank, Irene, M. *The Silk Road—A History*. New York: Facts on File Publishing, 1986.

Gladwin, Harold S. *Men out of Asia*. New York: McGraw-Hill, 1947.

Hamilton, E. J. *American Treasure and the Price Revolution in Spain*. New York: Octagon, 1965.

Hanke, Lewis. *The Spanish Struggle for Justice in the Conquest*. Boston: Little, Brown, 1965.

Hemming, John. *The Conquest of the Incas*. New York: Harcourt, Brace, Jovanovich, 1970.

Heyerdaho, Thor. *Early Man and The Ocean*. Garden City: Doubleday, 1979.

——. *Easter Island—The Mystery Solved*. New York: Random House, 1989.

Howarth, David, A. *Panama–Four Hundred Years of Dreams and Cruelty*. New York: McGraw Hill, 1966.

Irving, Washington. *Conquest of Granada*. New York and London: Newstead, Abbey, Abbotsford, N.d.

Kendall, Ann. *Everyday Life of the Incas*. New York: Dorsett Press, 1989.

Keyes, Frances P. *The Land of Stones and Saints*. New York: Hawthorne, 1961.

Kirkpatric, F. A. *The Spanish Conquistadores*. London: A and C Black, Ltd., 1934.

Kubler, George. *The Art and Architecture of Ancient America*. New York: Penguin, 1984.

La Barre, Weston. *The Aymara Indians of the Lake Titicaca Plateau*. New York: American Author's Association, 1948.

Lanning, Edward. P. *Peru Before the Incas*. Englewood Cliffs & Prentice-Hall, 1967.

Macgowan and Hester. *Early Man in the New World*. N.p., n.d.

MacNeish, Richard. *Early Man in the Andes*. N.p: Scientific American Assc., 1971.

Mariejol. Jean Hippolyte. *The Spain of Ferdinand and Isabella*. New Brunswick: Rutgers University Press, 1961.

Markham, Clements R. *A History of Peru*. Chicago: C. H. Sergal and Co., 1982.

——. *The Travels of Peter de Cieza de Leon*. London: Maggs Bros., London, 1907.

Mason, J. Alden. *The Ancient Civilizations of Peru*. New York: Penguin, 1988.

McBride, George, McC. *Chile—Land and Society*. New York: American Geographical Soc., 1936.

McIntyre, Loren. *The Incredible Incas and Their Timeless Land*. Washington, D.C.: National Geographic, 1977.

Means, Philip A. *Fall of the Inca Empire*. New York: Gordian Press, 1964.

——. *Ancient Civilizations of the Andes*. New York: Scribner's and Sons, 1931.

Merriman, R. B. *The Rise of the Spanish Empire in the Old World and the New*. New York: Macmillan, 1918–34.

Moorman, John., *History of the Franciscan Order*. Oxford: Claredon Press, 1968.

Morison, Samuel E. *Admiral of the Ocean Sea*. Camden: Atlantic, Little, Brown, 1942.

Neuberger, Albert. *The Technical Arts and Sciences of the Ancients*. New York: Barnes and Noble, 1930.

Miller. *Castles and The Crown*. N.p., n.d.

Montesinos, Fernando. *Memorias Antiquas Historicas del Peru*. N.p., n.d.

Nordeenskiold, Baron Erland. *Origin of the Indian Civilization in South America*. Toronto: University of Toranto Press, N.d.

Parry, J. H. *Europe and a Wider World—1415–1715*. Berkley: University of California Press, 1953.

Pizarro, Francisco. *From Panama to Peru, the Conquest of Peru by the Pizarros* (Huntington Library—100 copies only). Pasadena: Huntington Library, 1925.

Pizarro, Pedro. *Relation of the Discovery and Conquest of the Kingdom of Peru.* New York: Cortes Society, 1921.

Posnansky, Arthur. *Tihuanacu: Cradle of American Man.* New York: J.J. Augustin, 1945, 1958.

Prescott, William, H. *History of the Conquest of Peru.* New York: G. Routledge and Sons, 1847.

———. *The World of Incas.* Geneva: Edition Minerva, 1970.

———. *Rise and Decline of the Spanish Empire.* New York: J. Messner, 1948.

———. *History of the Reign of Ferdinand and Isabella.* Philadelphia: P. McKay, 1893.

Raymond, LeBlanc, J. *Gold Leaf Techniques.* Cincinnati: Signs of the Times Publications, 1980.

Reiche, Maria. *Mystery of the Desert.* N.p.: Stuttgart-Vaihingen, 1968.

Richards. *Precious Metals in the Late Medieval and Early Modern Worlds.* Durham: Carolina Academic Press, 1983.

Rowe, John H. *Introduction to the Archaeology of Cuzco.* Cambridge: Harvard University Press, 1939.

Sachar, Abram Leon. *A History of the Jews.* New York: Knopf, 1930, 1964.

Salas, Eugenio Pereira. *History of Art in the Reign of Chile.* Madrid, 1851.

Sancho, Pedro. *An Account of the Conquest of Peru.* New York: Cortes Society, 1917.

Shay, Frank. *Incredible Pizarro.* New York: Mohawk Press, 1932.

Squires, E. George. *Peru, Land of the Incas.* New York: American Press, 1973.

Stierlin, Henri. *Art of the Incas.* New York: Rizzoli, 1984.

Tibesar, Antonine. *Franciscan Beginnings in Colonial Peru.* N.p., n.d.

Tooley, R. V. *Maps and Mapmakers.* New York: Bonanza

151

Books, 1949.

Trevor, Davies R. *The Golden Age of Spain—1501–1621*. New York: St. Martin's Press, 1967.

Tschiffley, Aime Felix. *Coricancha (Garden of Gold)*. Cambridge: Harvard University Press, 1943.

Vargas Llosa, Mario. *The Storyteller*. New York: Farrar, Strauss, and Giroux, 1989.

Varner, John. *El Inca—The Life and Times of de la Vega*. Austin: University of Texas Press, 1968.

Von Hagen, Victor W. *Highway of the Sun*. New York: Mentor, 1955.

——. *Realm of the Incas*. New York: Mentor, 1957, 1961.

——. *Guide to Sacsahuaman, the Fortress of Cuzco*. New York: Graphic Society Publishing, 1965.

Von Hunboldt. *Researches Concerning the Institutions and Monuments of the Ancient Inhabitants of America*. N.p., n.d.

Werlich, David. P. *Peru—A Short History*. Carbondale: South Illinois University Press, 1978.

Wilder, Thornton. *The Bridge of San Luis Rey*. New York: Penguin, 1927.

Wilford, John N. *The Mapmakers*. New York: Knopf, 1981.

Index